"Creativity is the flame that lights the path to the expression of the soul, and its colorful strokes transform the world into a work of art."

"Dedicated to my beloved children (Enzo Gabriel and Geovana) and to my dear husband Gilvan. To you, who are the stars that shine in my life, I dedicate this coloring book. Thank you for being my constant source of inspiration, for awakening creativity in me and for filling my days with love and joy. Each page of this book is an invitation to color our memories, our precious moments together. Through colors and lines, I want to express how grateful I am to have you by my side, sharing laughter, hugs and dreams. And to everyone who will be coloring these pages, thank you for joining us on this journey of creativity and love. That each stroke and brushstroke represents the unique beauty within you, and that these colorful diamonds that emerge are reflections of your separate souls. May this book be a constant reminder of our union, our bonds and all the love that surrounds us. May we create together, share our cores and spread joy wherever we go

. With all my love, Eliana Lima

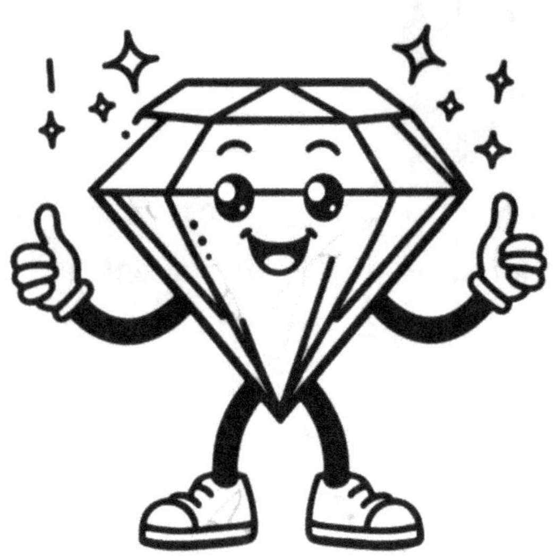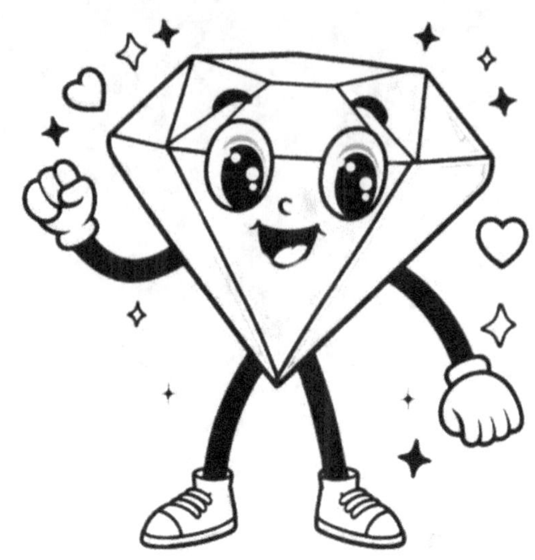

This book belongs to:

____

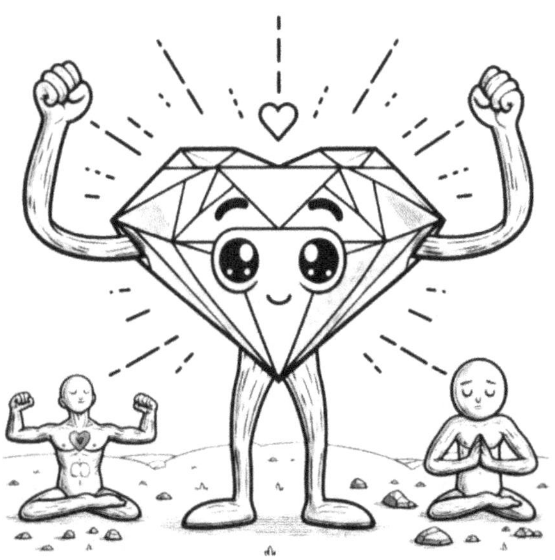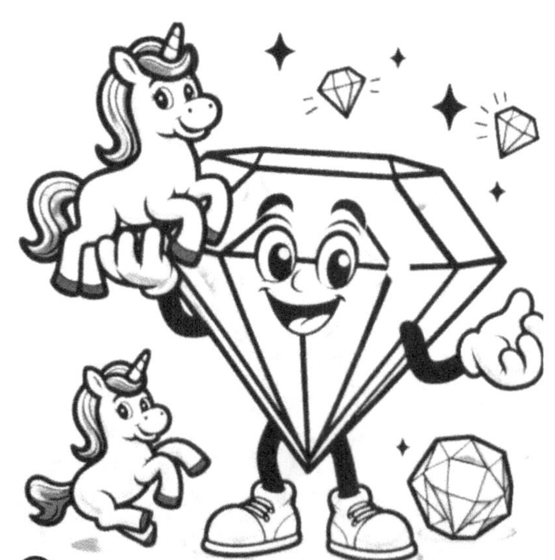

Test Colors on the Page

Once upon a time, in a distant kingdom, there was a very special diamond called Brilliant. He was known for his beauty and brilliance exceptional, but there was something that differentiated him from the others diamonds: he possessed a unique soul.

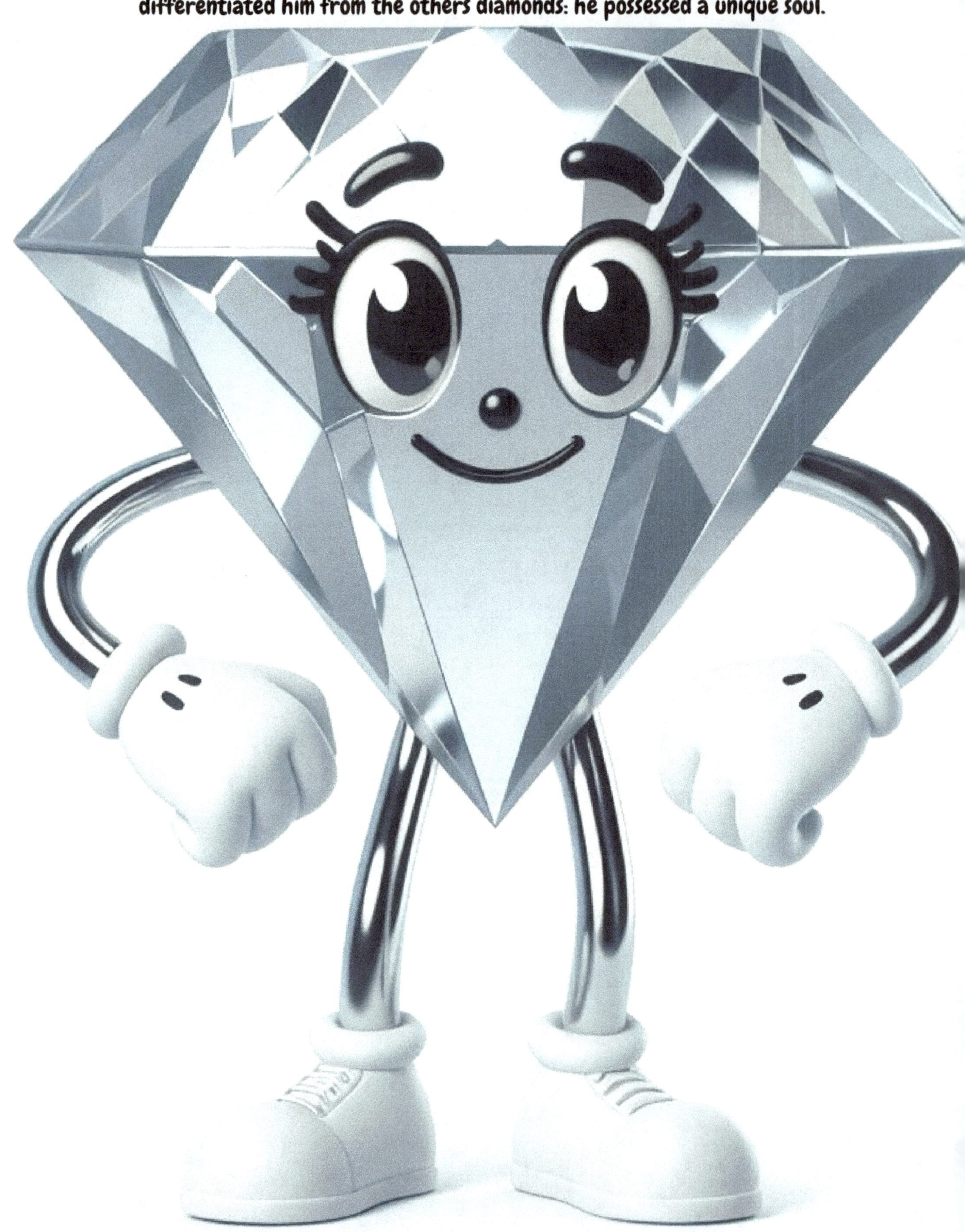

Unlike ordinary diamonds, Brilliant had the ability to feel emotions. However, there was a problem: he didn't I could understand what I felt. It left him confused and curious at the same time.

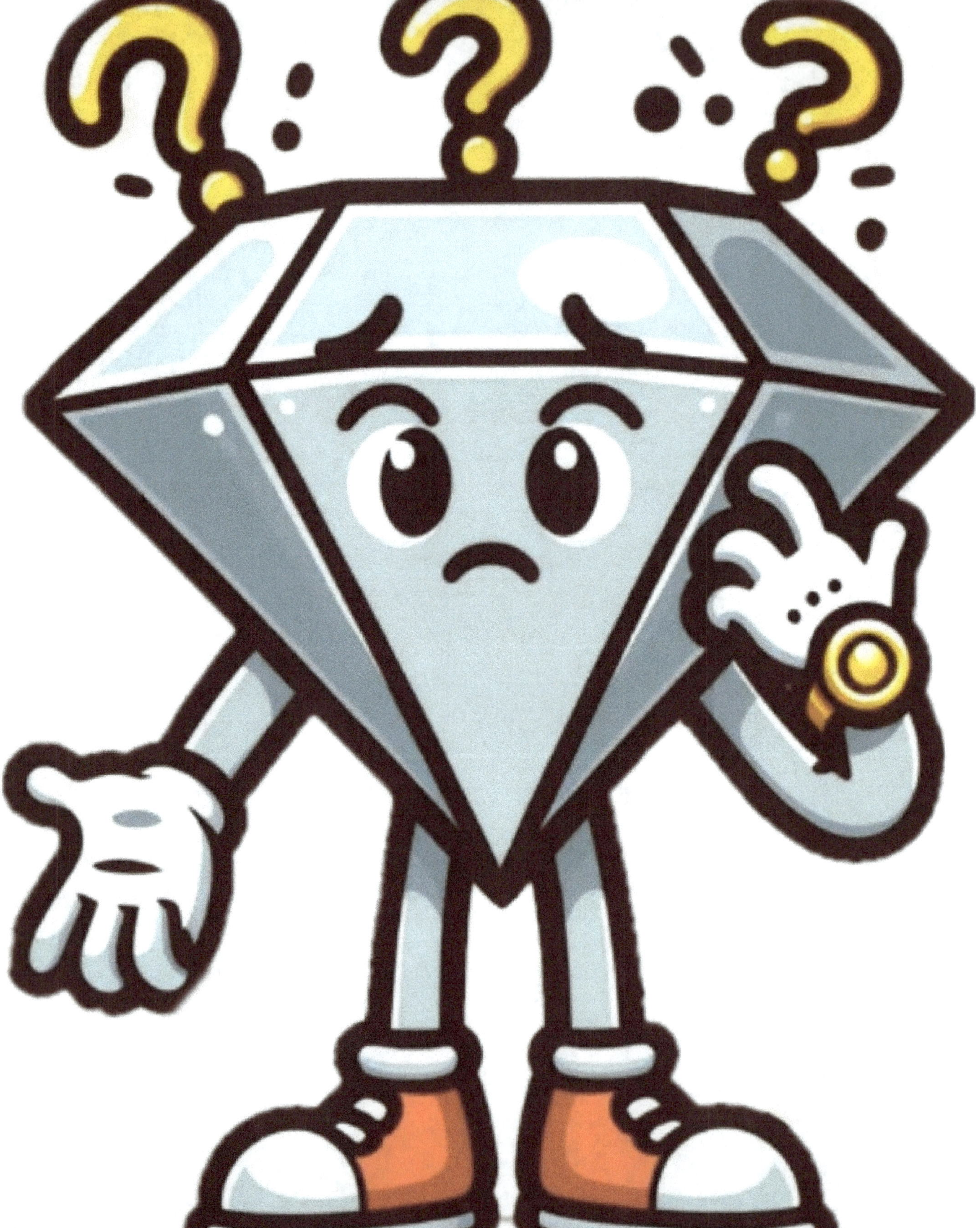

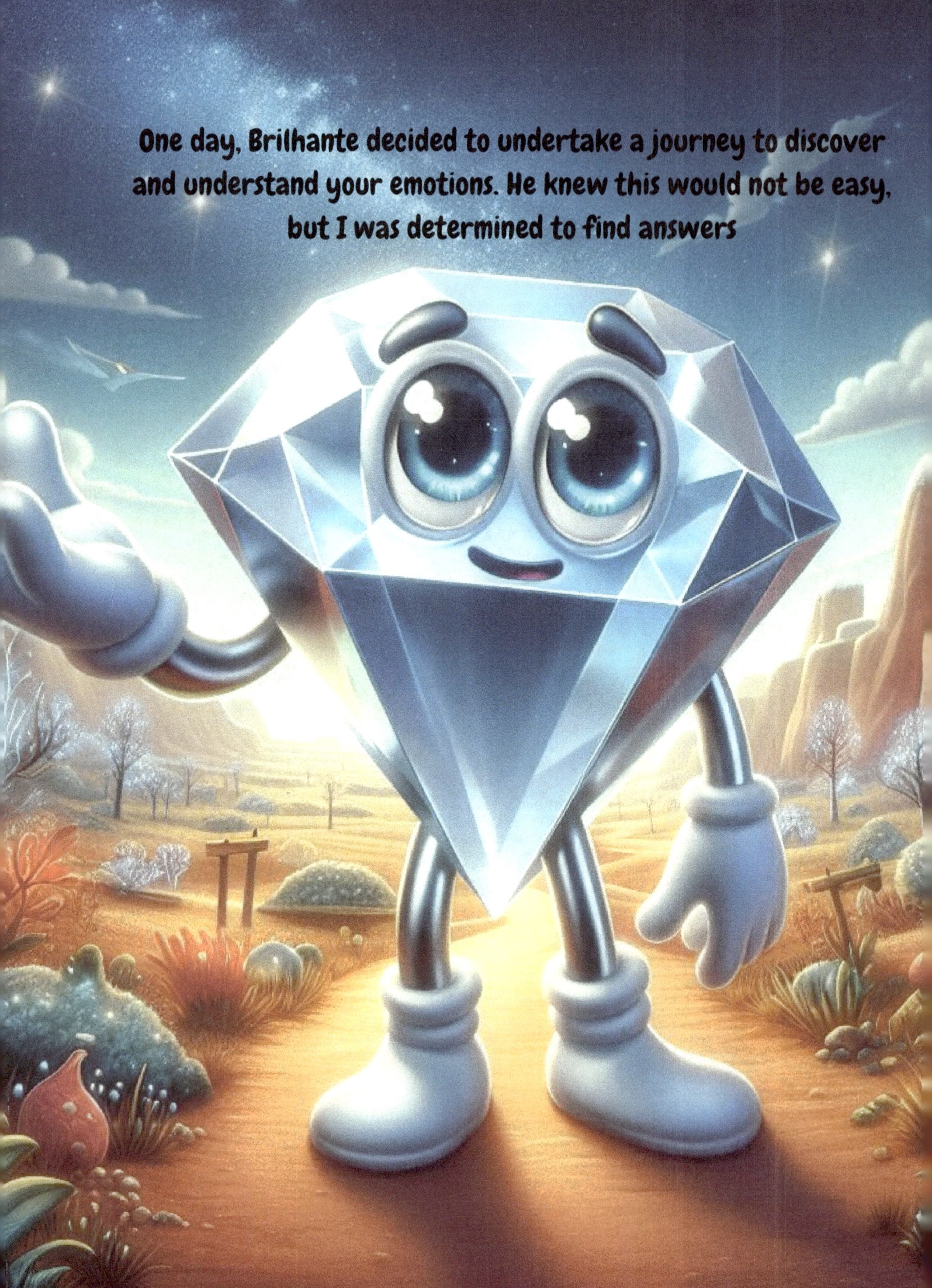

One day, Brilhante decided to undertake a journey to discover
and understand your emotions. He knew this would not be easy,
but I was determined to find answers

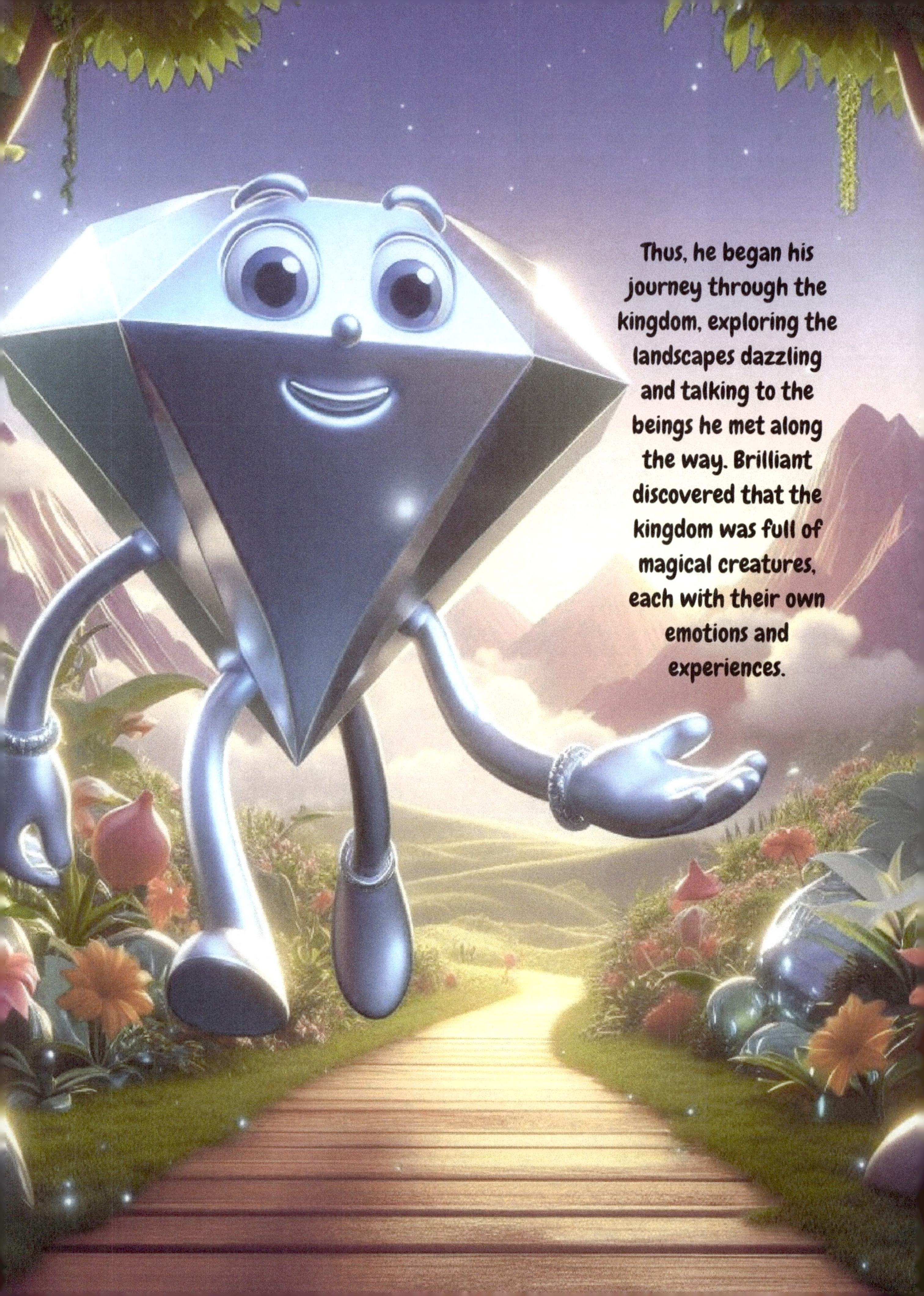

Thus, he began his journey through the kingdom, exploring the landscapes dazzling and talking to the beings he met along the way. Brilliant discovered that the kingdom was full of magical creatures, each with their own emotions and experiences.

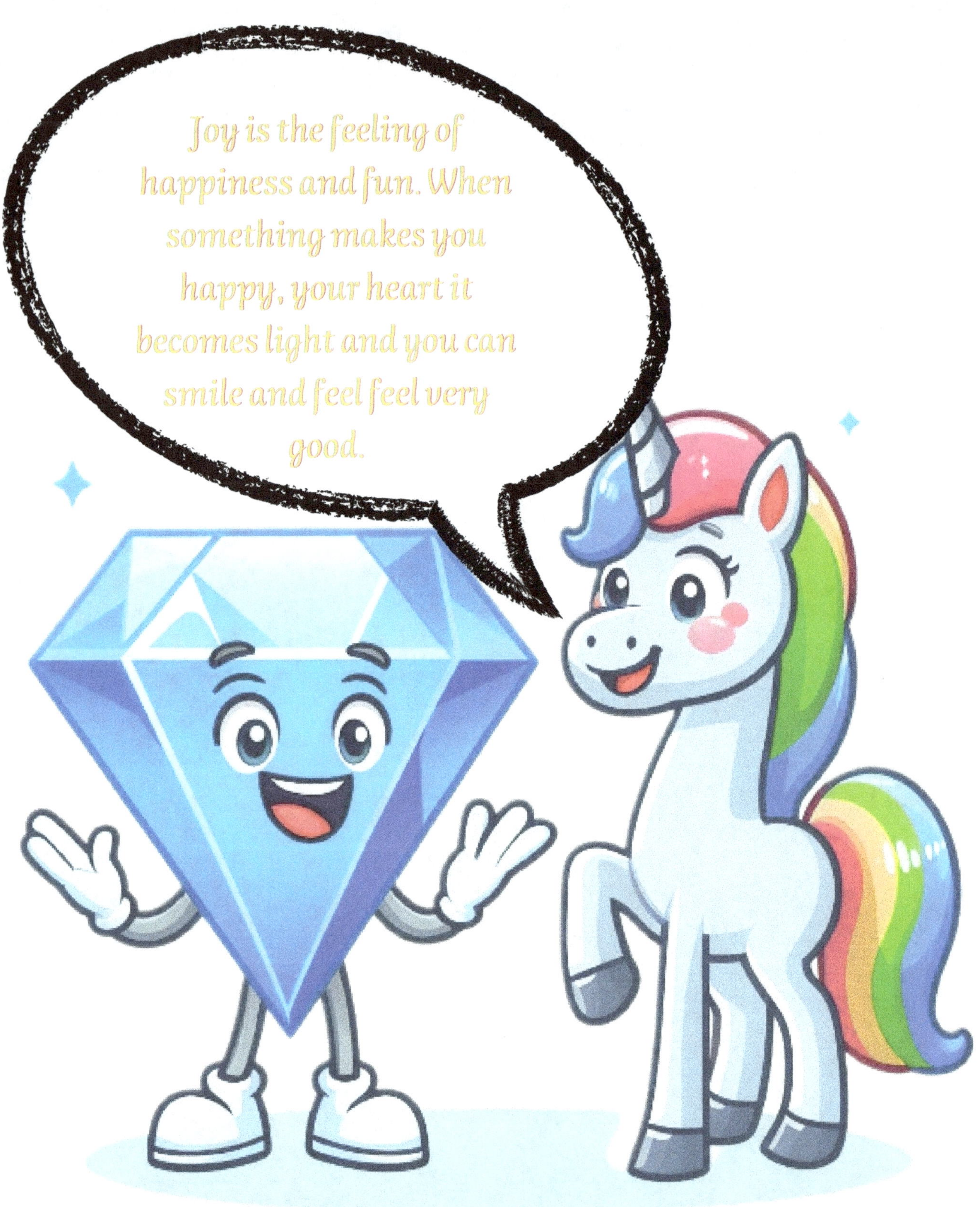

He met a unicorn named Rainbow, who taught him about joy and happiness. Brilliant felt a sense of warmth and lightness when learning about these emotions. He realized that joy was like a ray of sunlight that illuminated his heart

Let's color Brilliant! This way it will increase your joy..

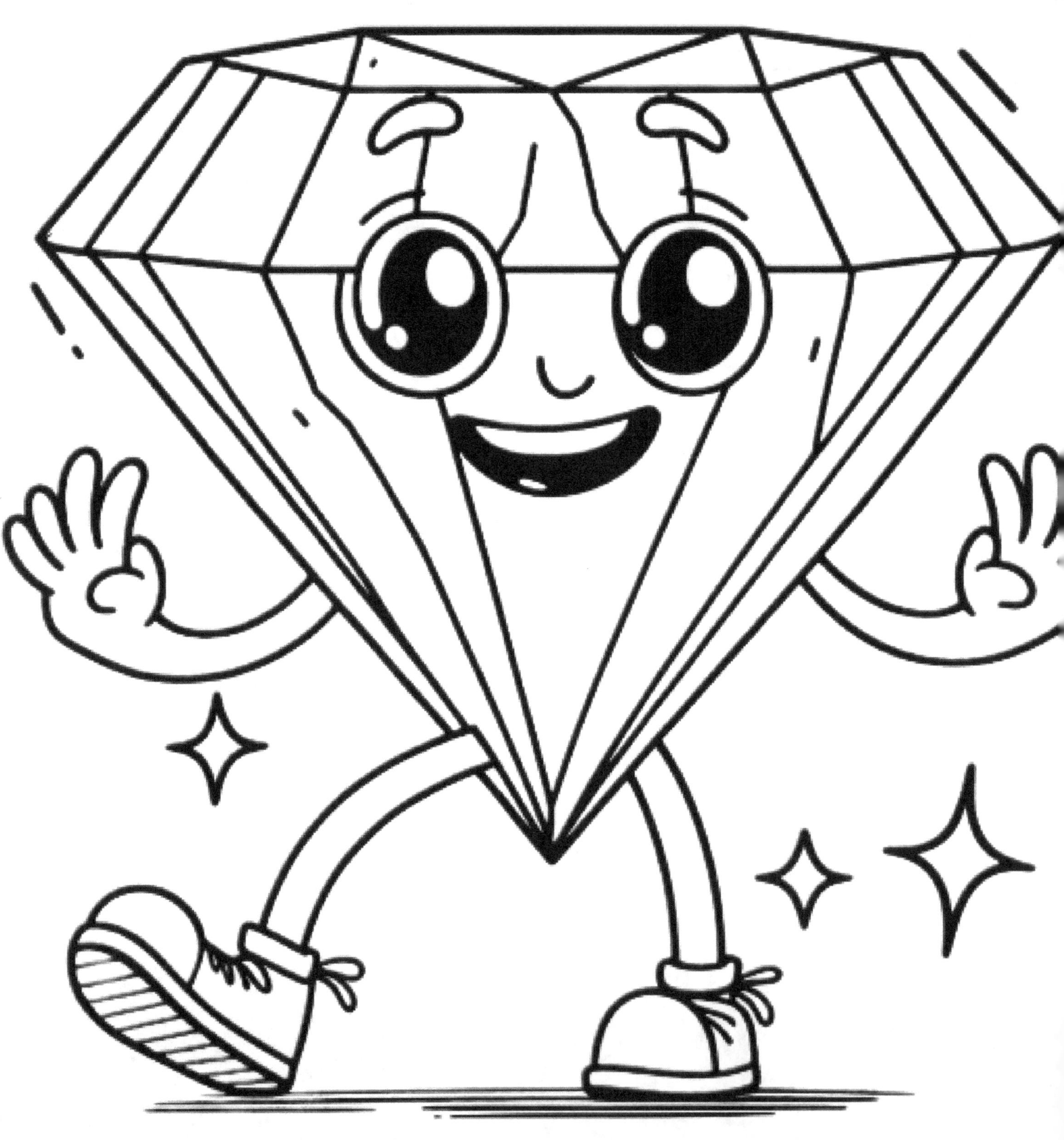

Let's color Brilliant! This way it will increase your joy..

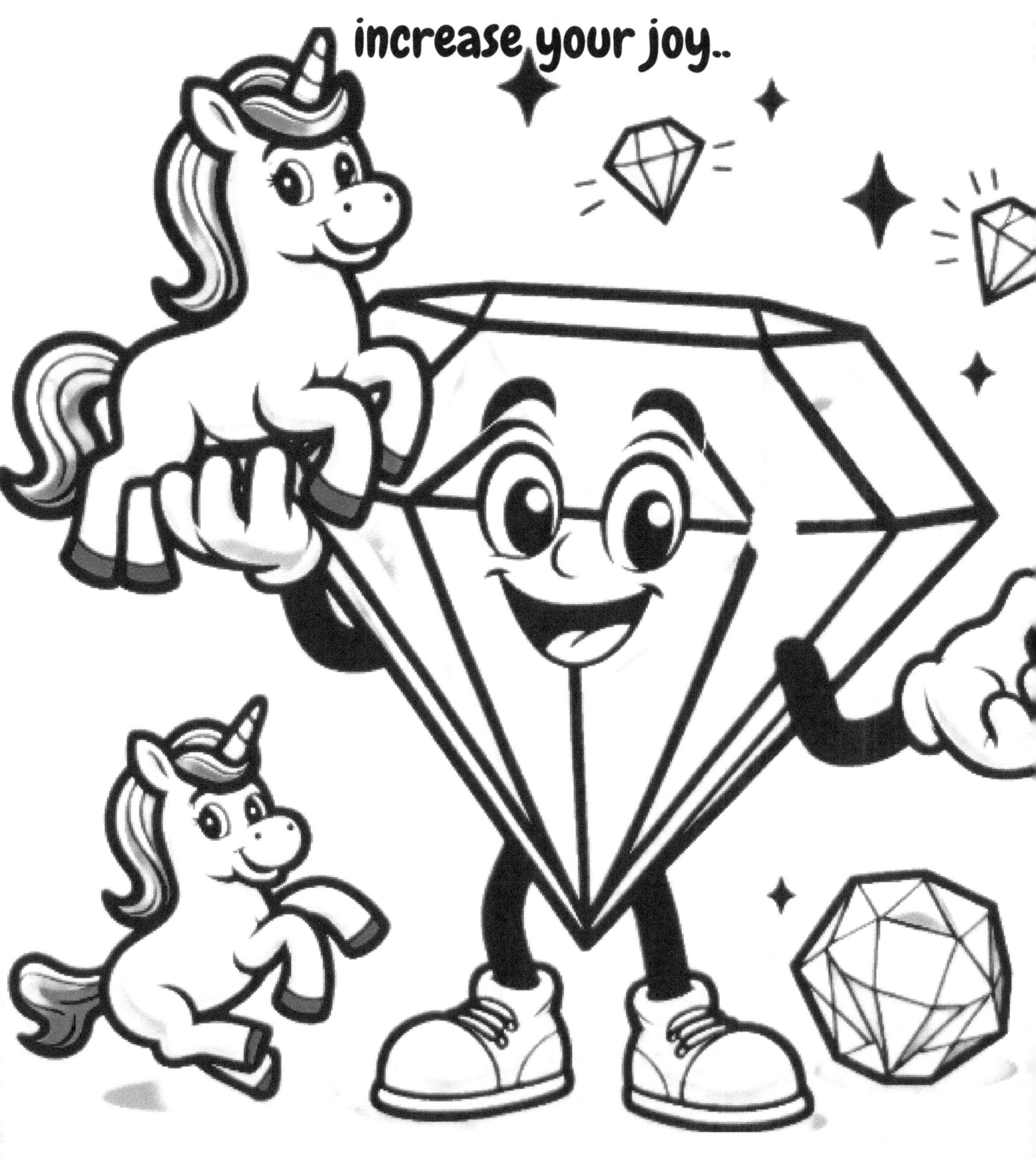

Let's color Brilliant! This way it will increase your joy..

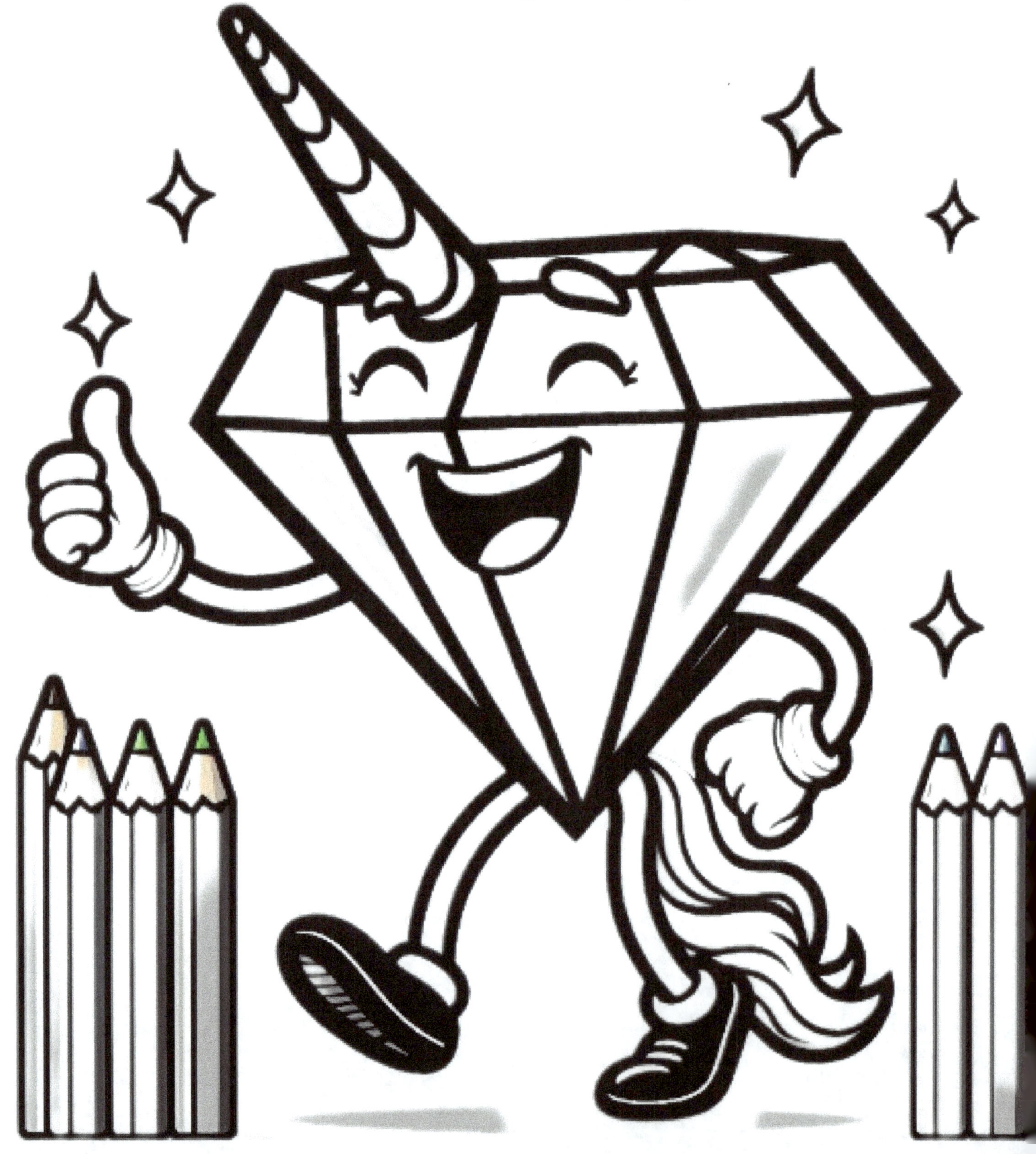

Let's color Brilliant! This way it will increase your joy..

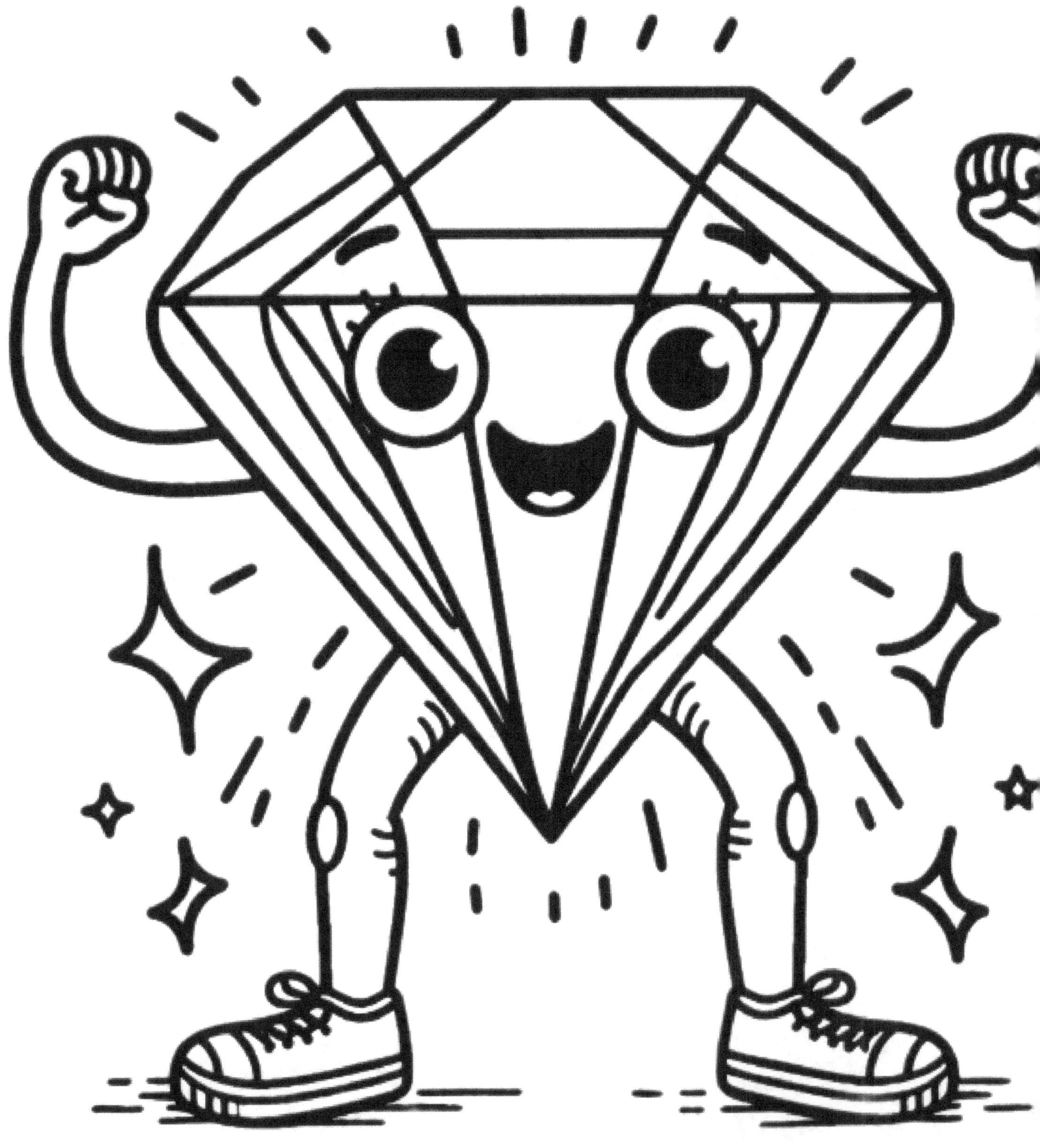

Let's color Brilliant! This way it will increase your joy..

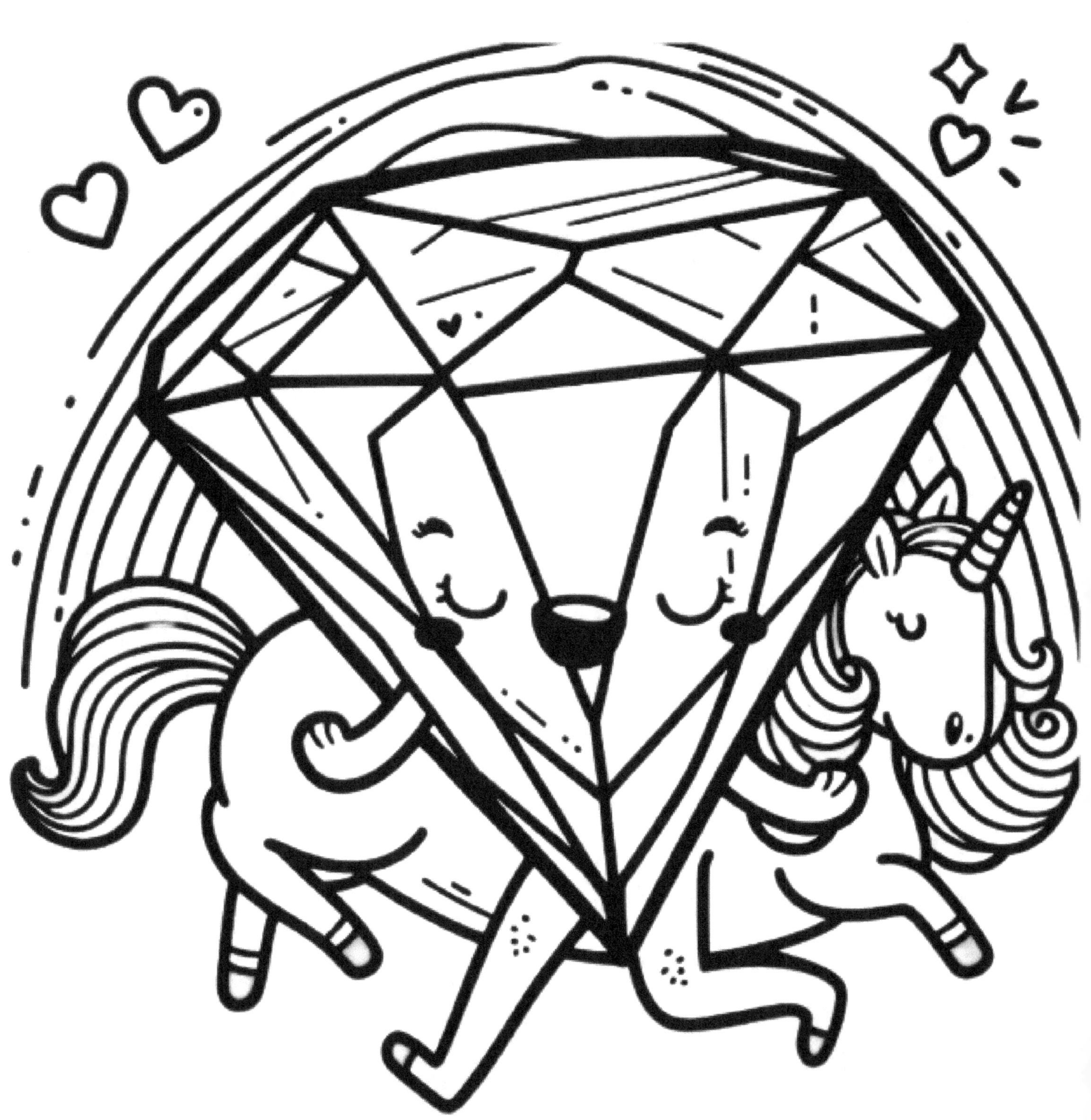

Let's color Brilliant! This way it will increase your joy..

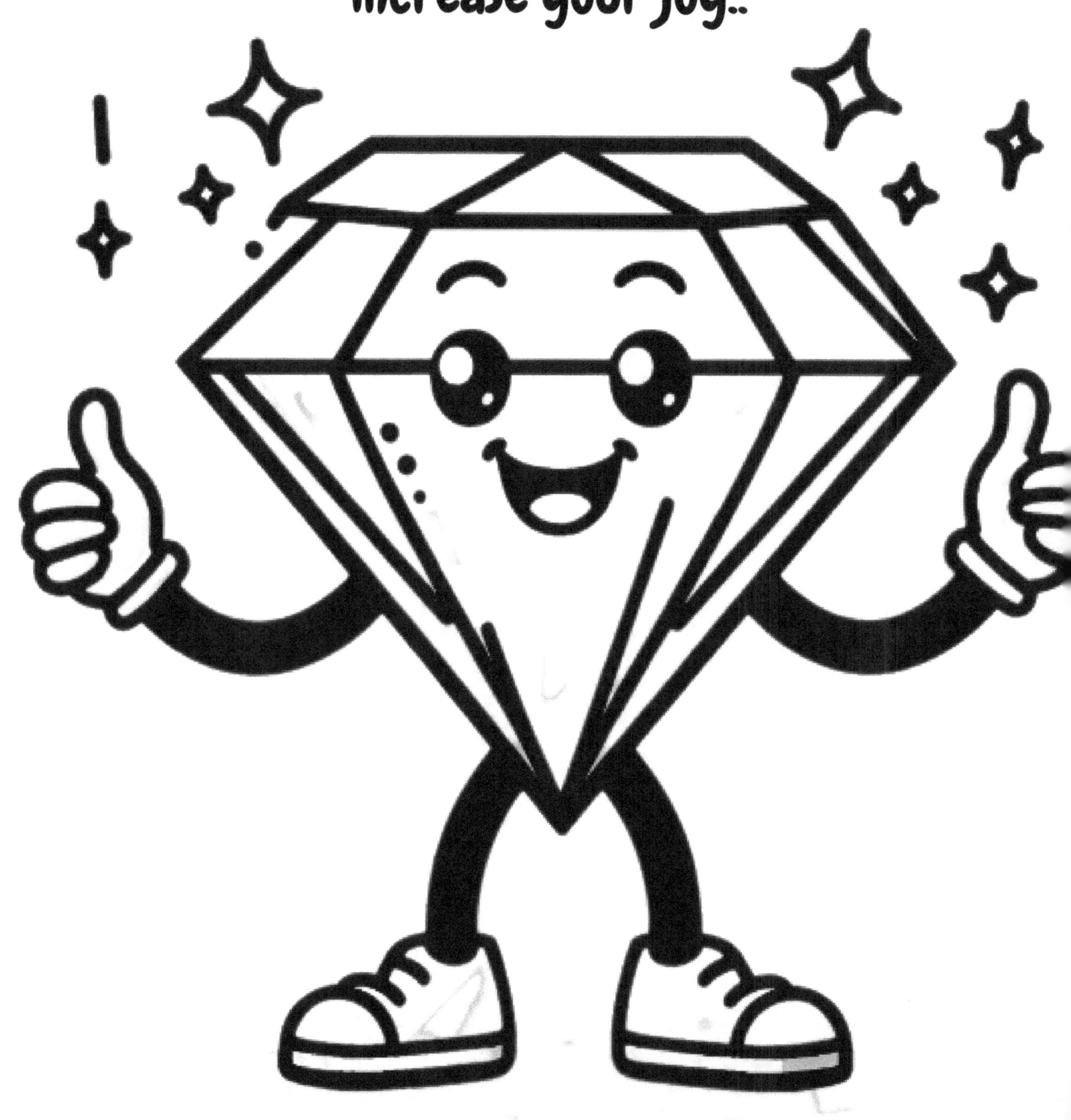

Thank you little friend, Brilhante He was happy that you shared your joy with him

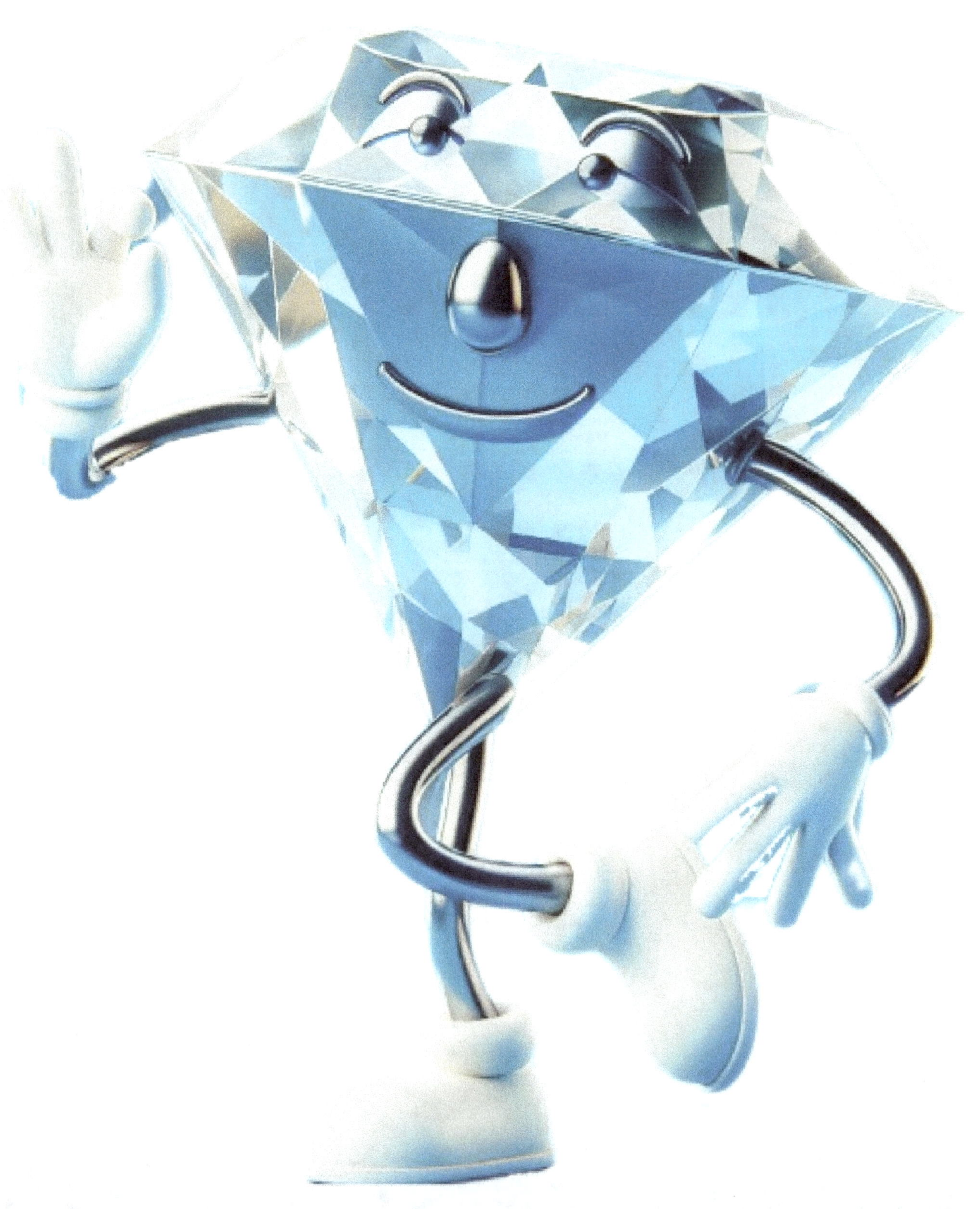

Perfect Brilliant is super happy! Now it is your turn: Draw a drawing that represents the day that you felt joy.

On her journey, Shiny also encountered a fairy named Melancholy, which showed him sadness and pain. Although these emotions were difficult to understand, Brilliant understood that they were part of life and that they helped value moments of joy even more.

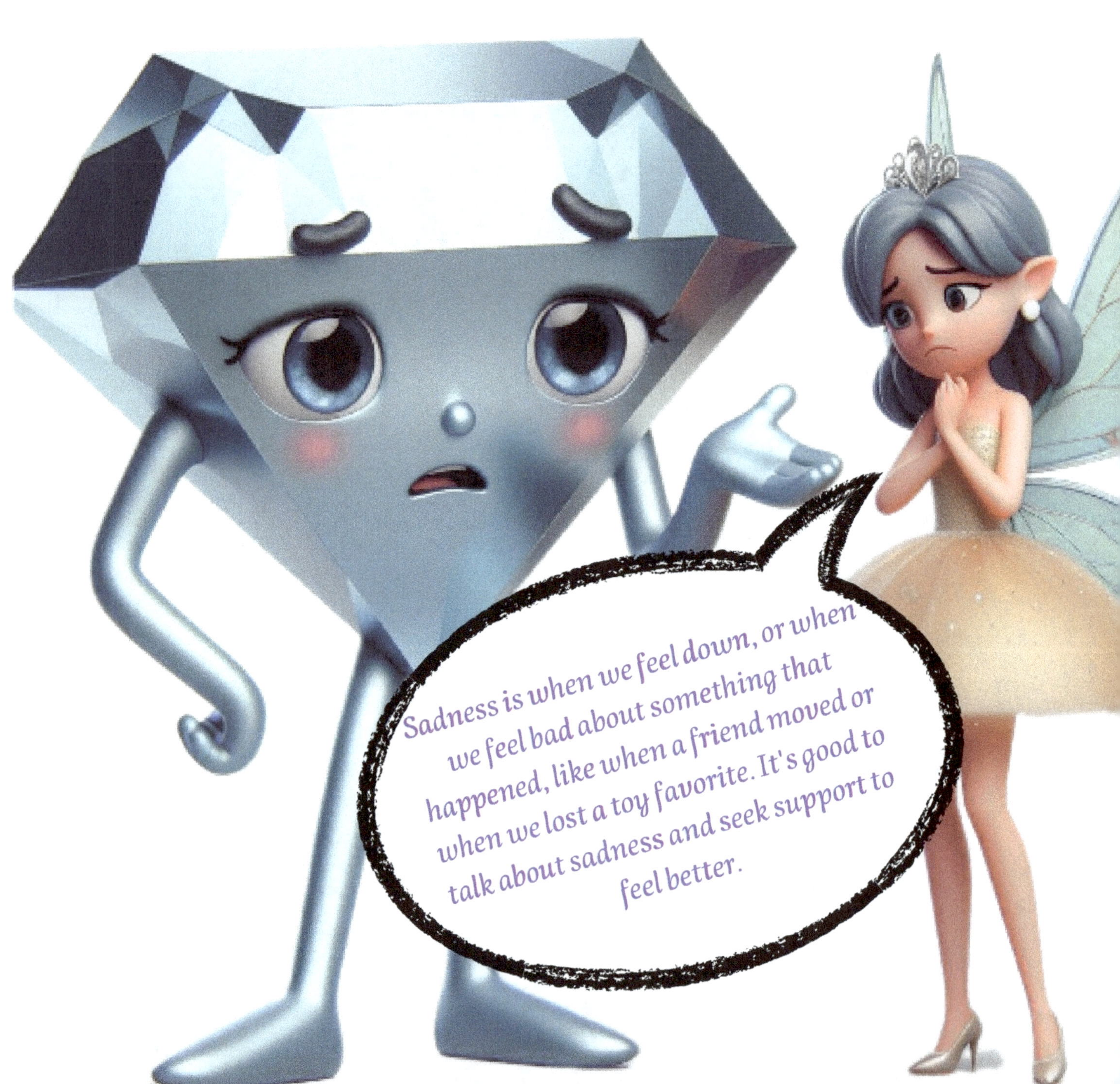

Let's color Brilliant! He is trying to understand the emotion
of sadness within him, he remembered the times he was sad.
A little color will help!

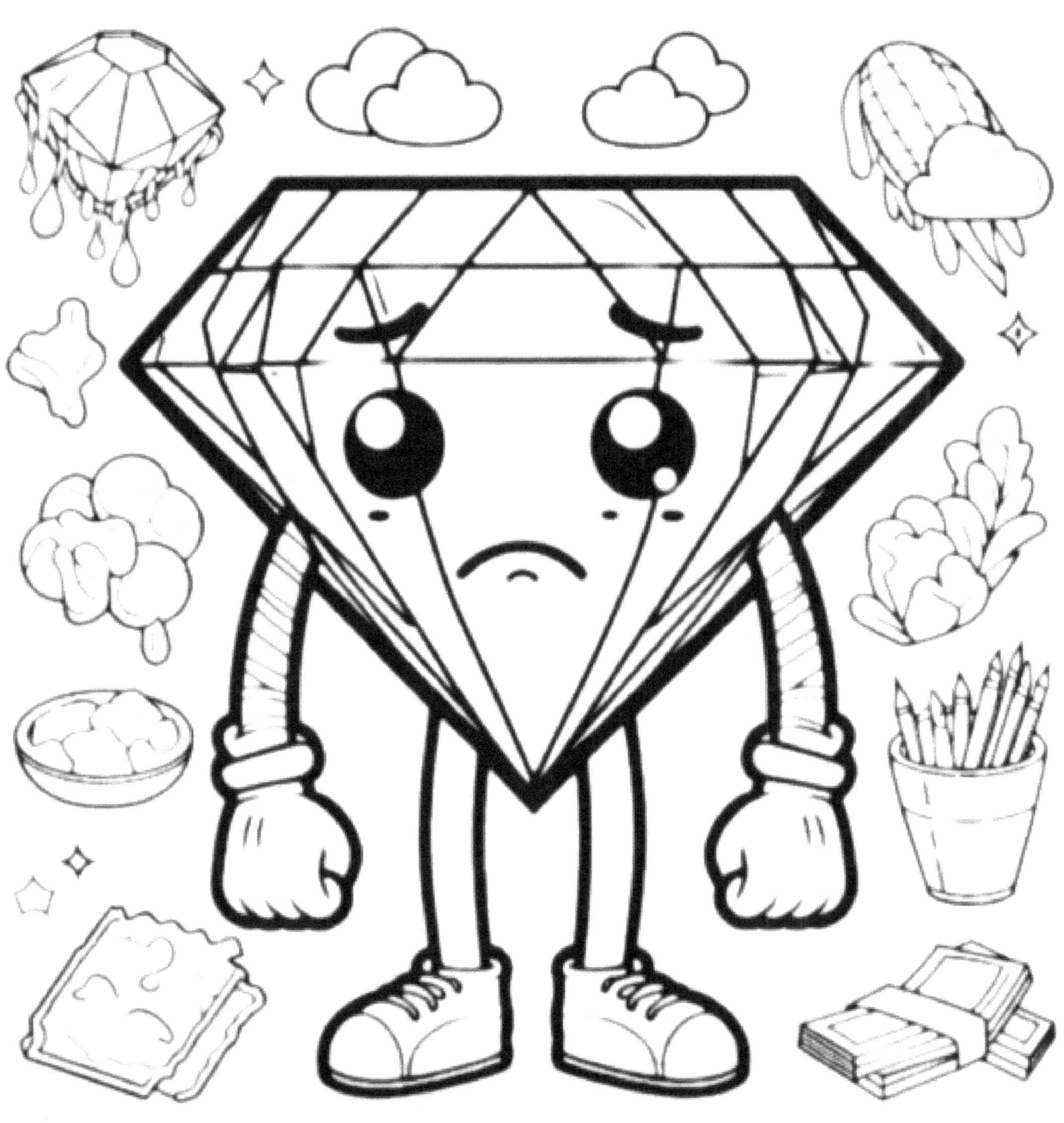

Let's color Brilliant! He is trying to understand the emotion
of sadness within him, he remembered the times he was sad.
A little color will help!

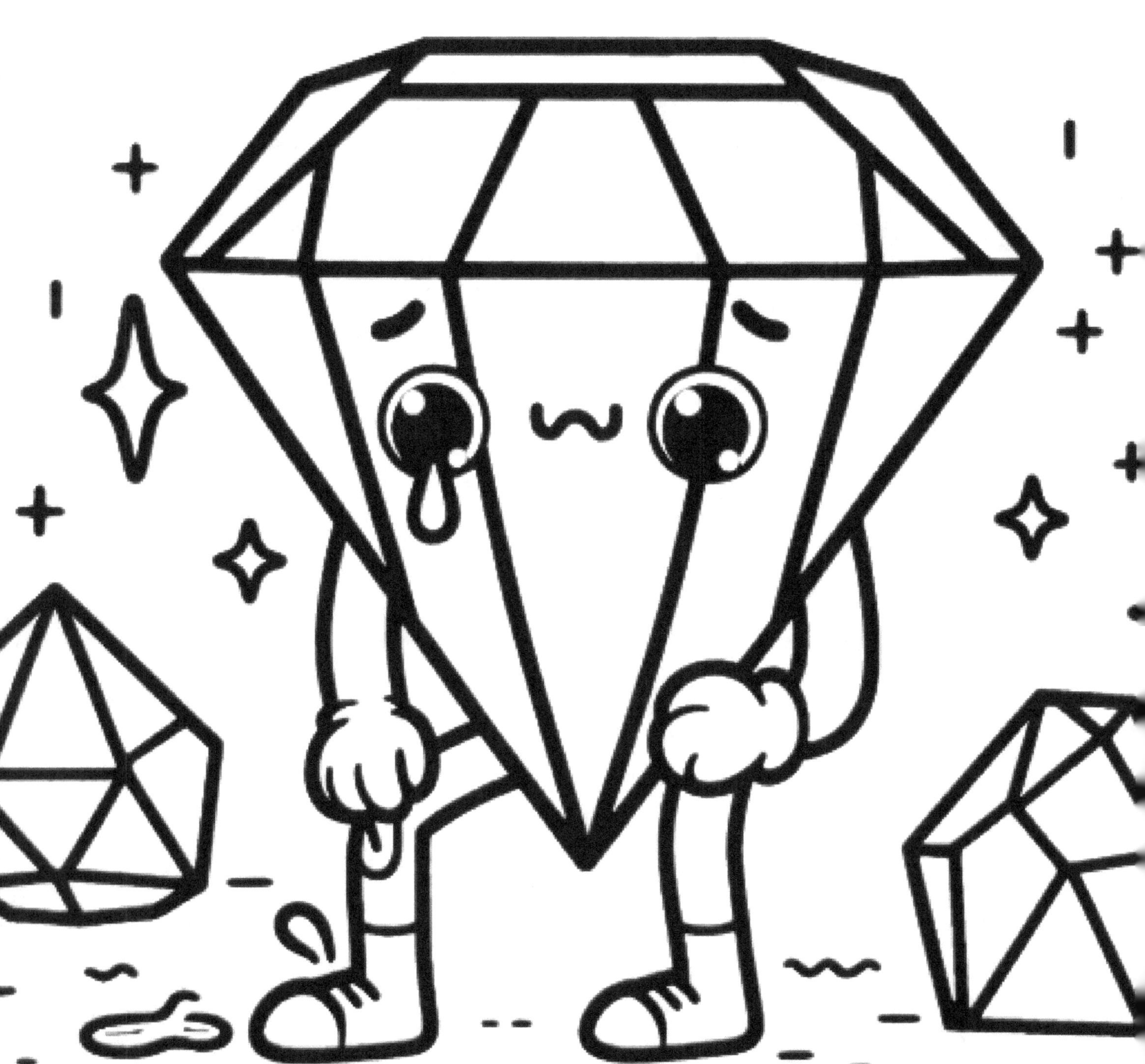

Let's color Brilliant! He is trying to understand the emotion
of sadness within him, he remembered the times he was sad.
A little color will help!

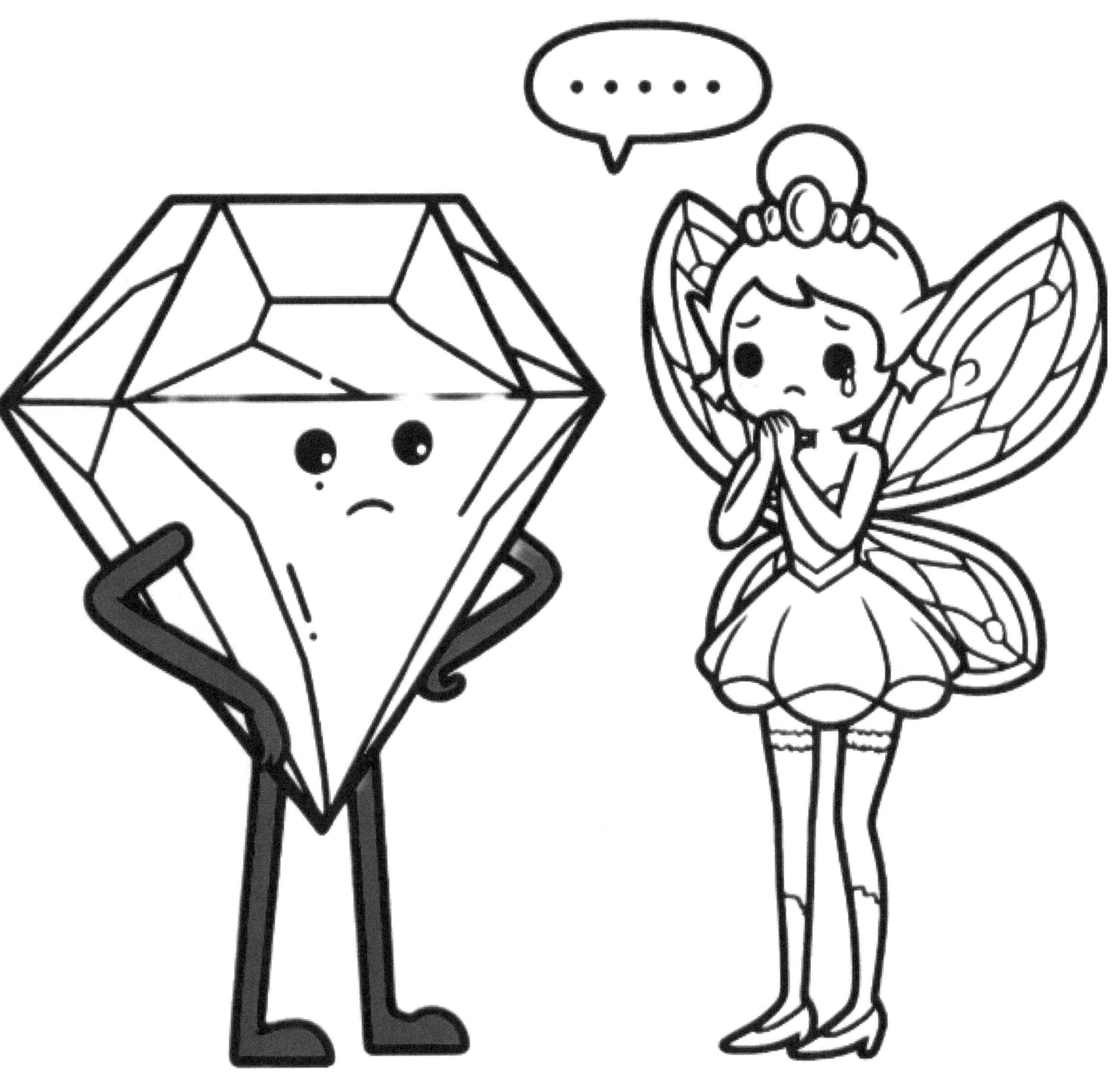

Let's color Brilliant! He is trying to understand the emotion of sadness within him, he remembered the times he was sad. A little color will help!

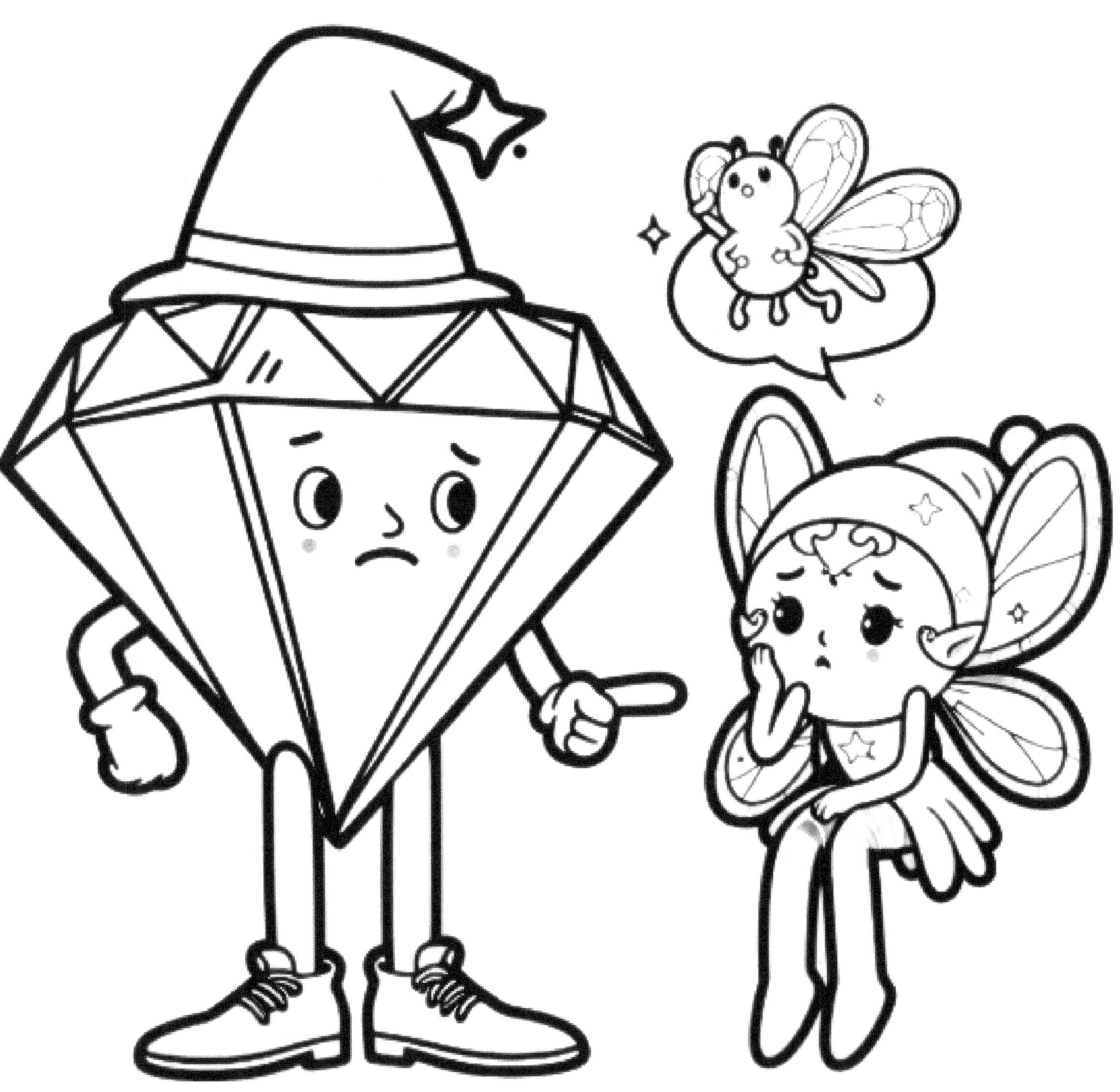

Let's color Brilliant! He is trying to understand the emotion
of sadness within him, he remembered the times he was sad.
A little color will help!

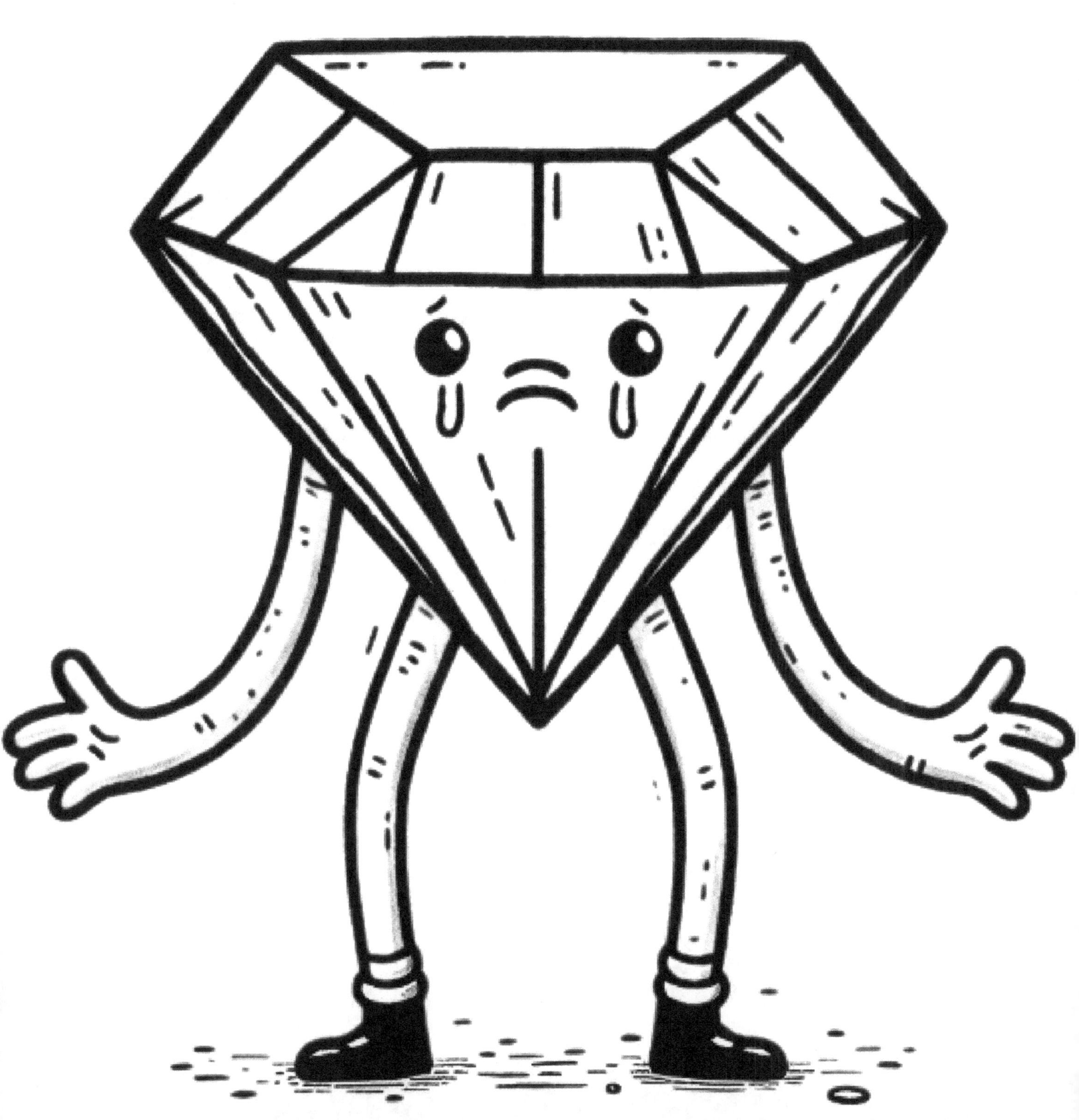

Let's color Brilliant! He is trying to understand the emotion of sadness within him, he remembered the times he was sad. A little color will help!

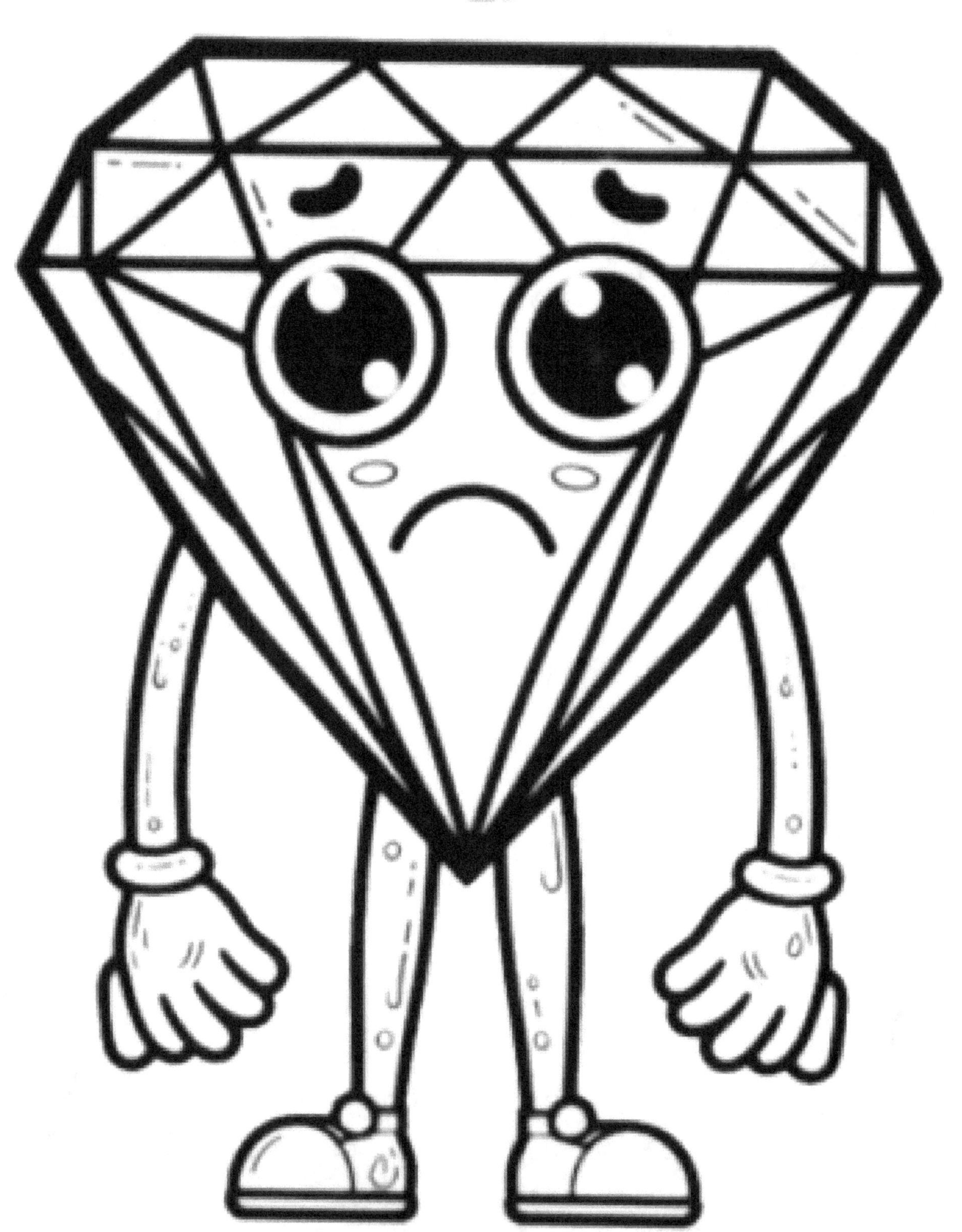

Wow, Brilliant managed to understand, The emotion of sadness. He is now happy, Thank you, little friend, for helping him!

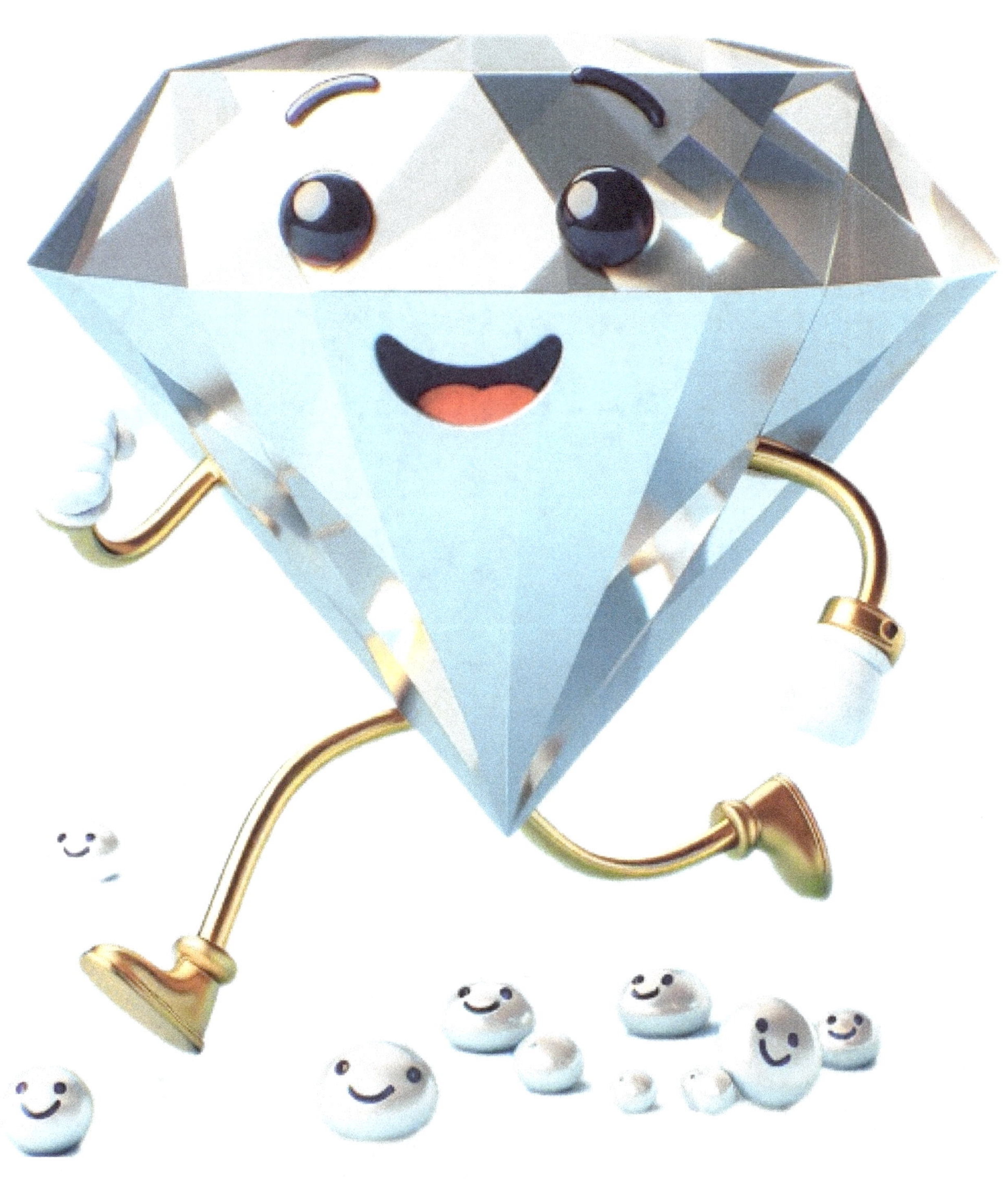

Brilliant is fine, now it's your turn! Draw a moment when you were sad and how did you react?

On his quest, Brilliant met a dragon named Fury, who showed him anger and frustration. These emotions were powerful and intense, and Brilhante realized that they were also part of who he was. The anger was like an erupting volcano, but he learned to understand why he felt angry.

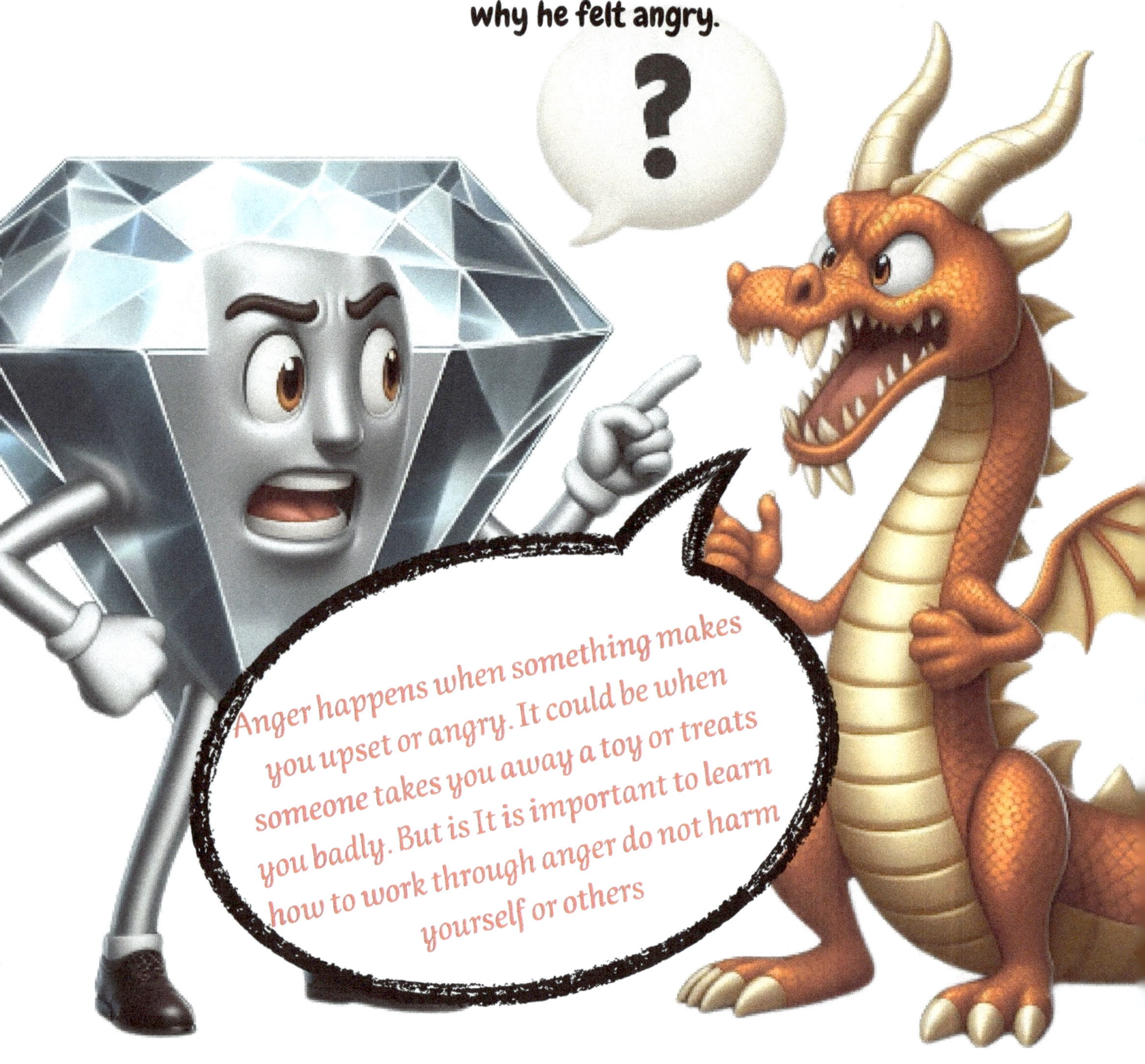

Let's color Brilliant, now he's understanding sometimes that he felt angry. Let's help him to calm down.

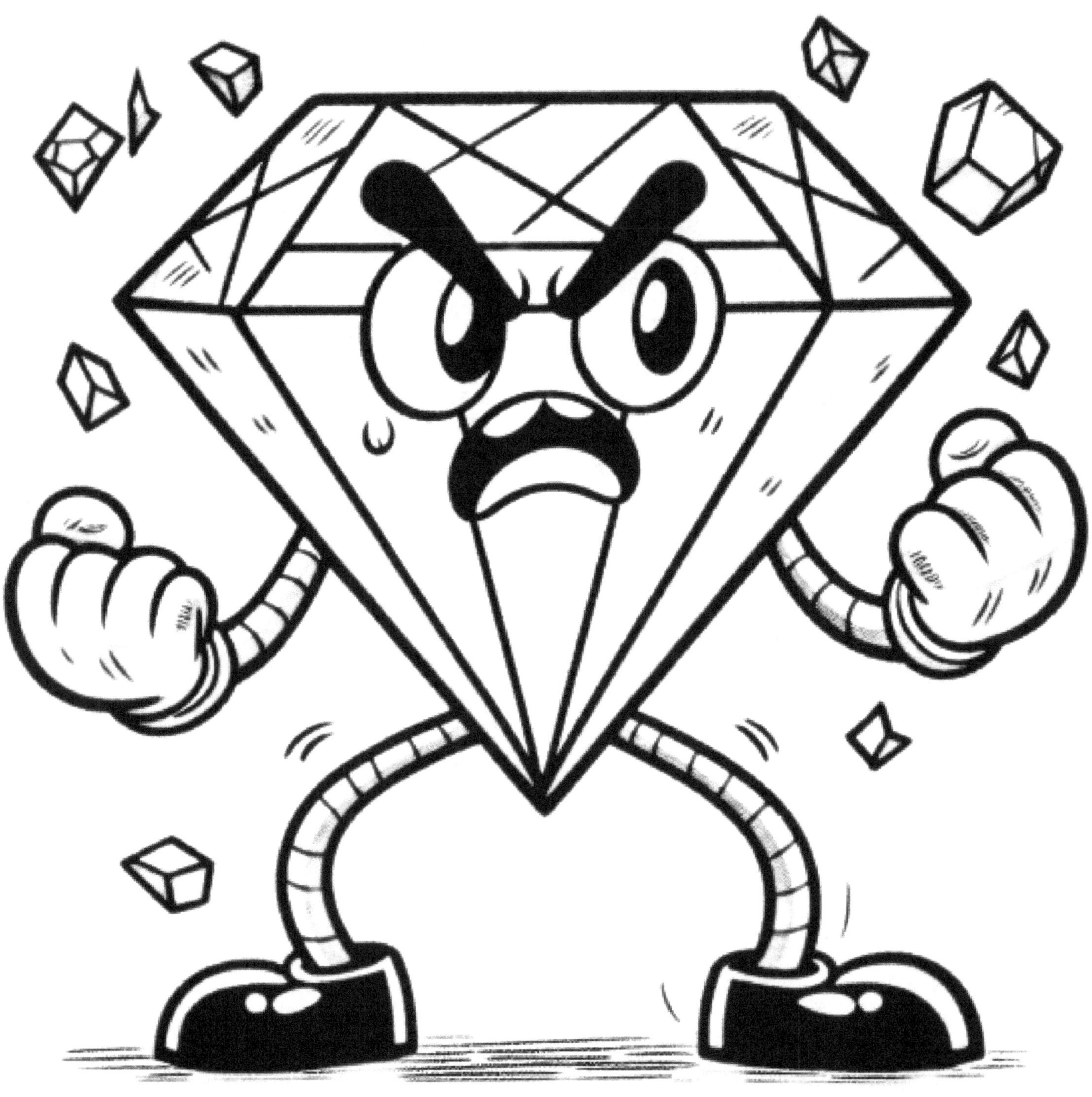

Let's color Brilliant, now he's understanding sometimes that he felt angry. Let's help him to calm down.

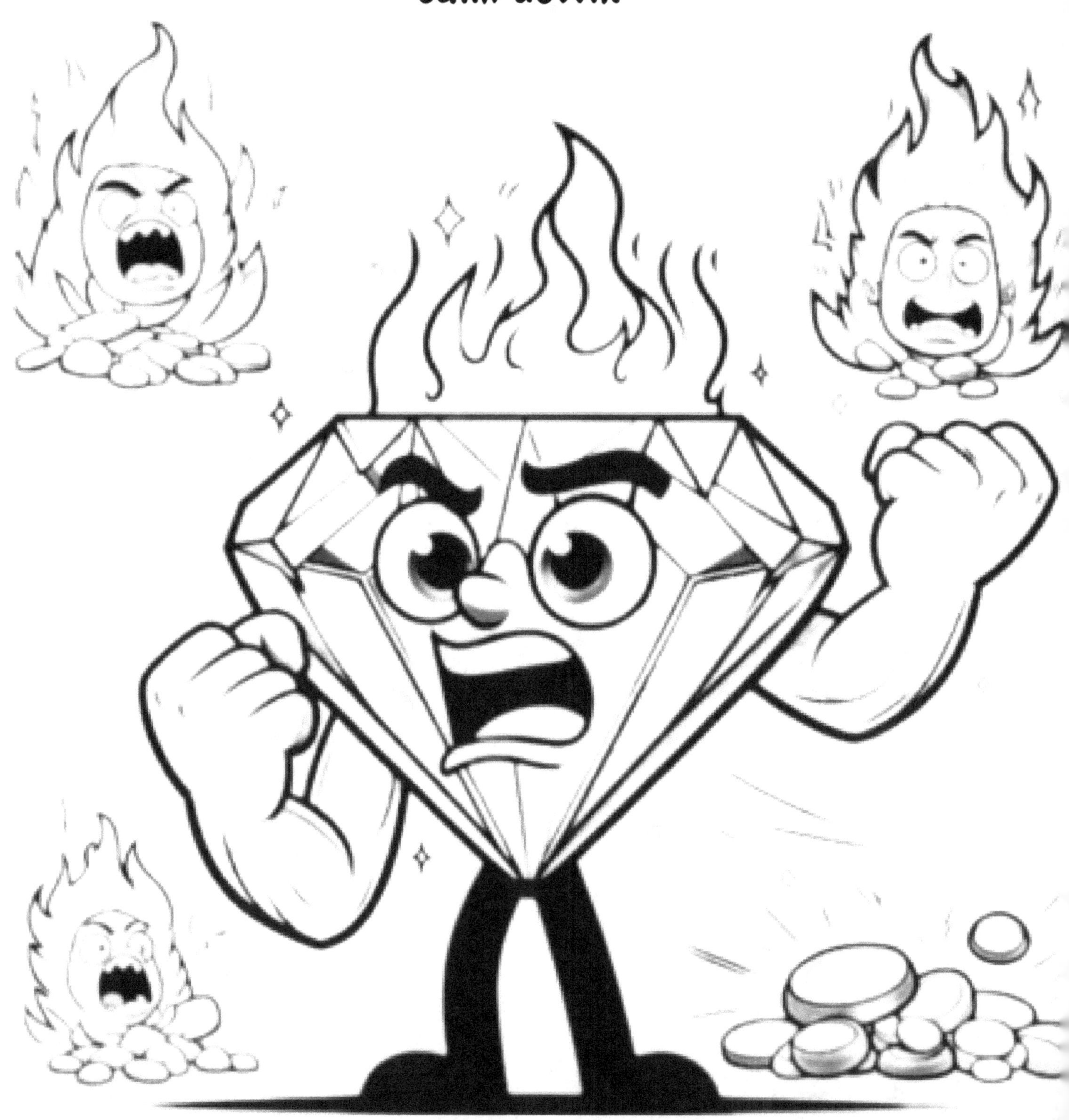

Let's color Brilliant, now he's understanding sometimes that he felt angry. Let's help him to calm down.

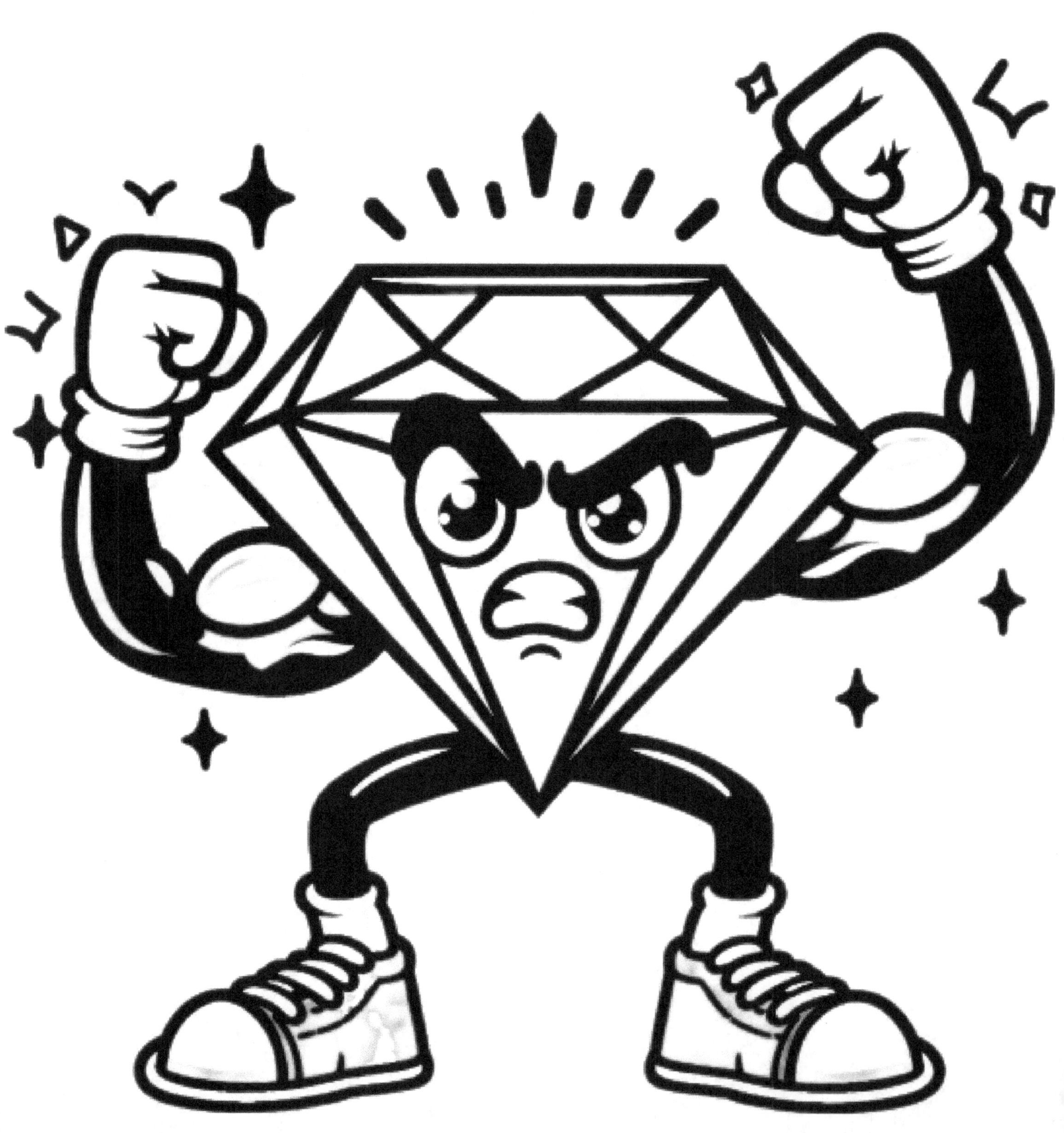

Let's color Brilliant, now he's understanding sometimes that he felt angry. Let's help him to calm down.

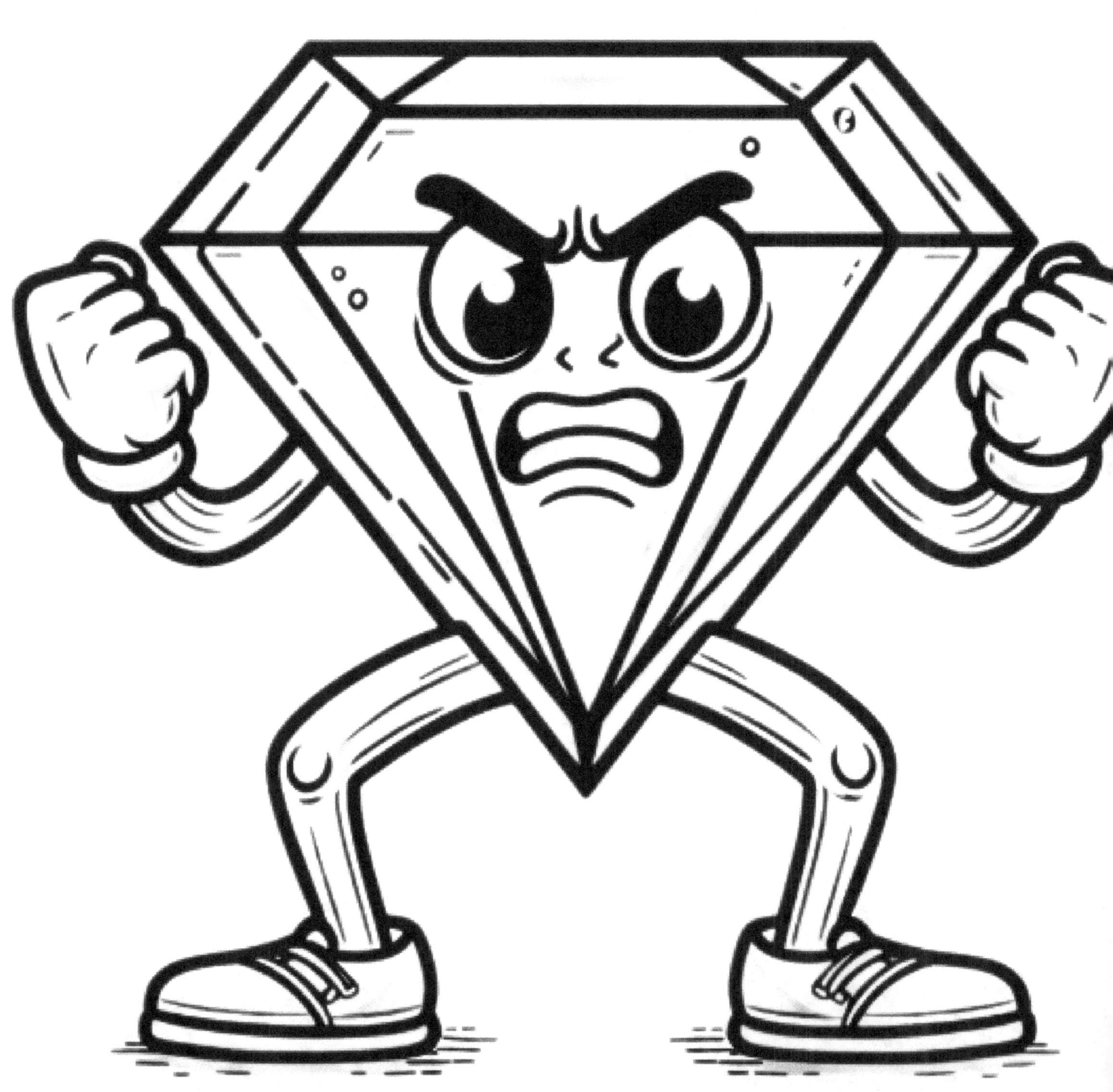

Let's color Brilliant, now he's understanding sometimes that he felt angry. Let's help him to calm down.

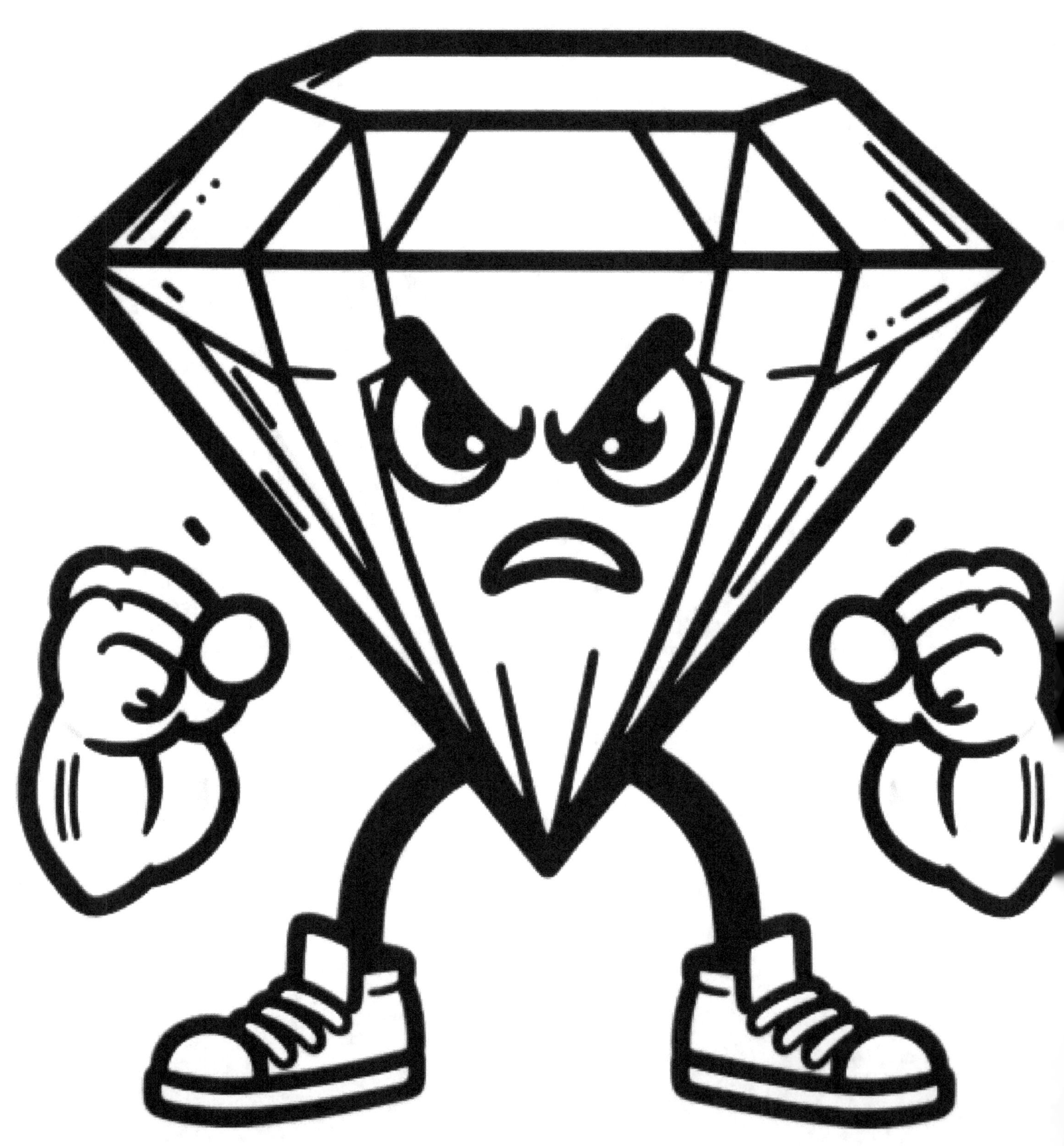

Let's color Brilliant, now he's understanding sometimes that he felt angry. Let's help him to calm down.

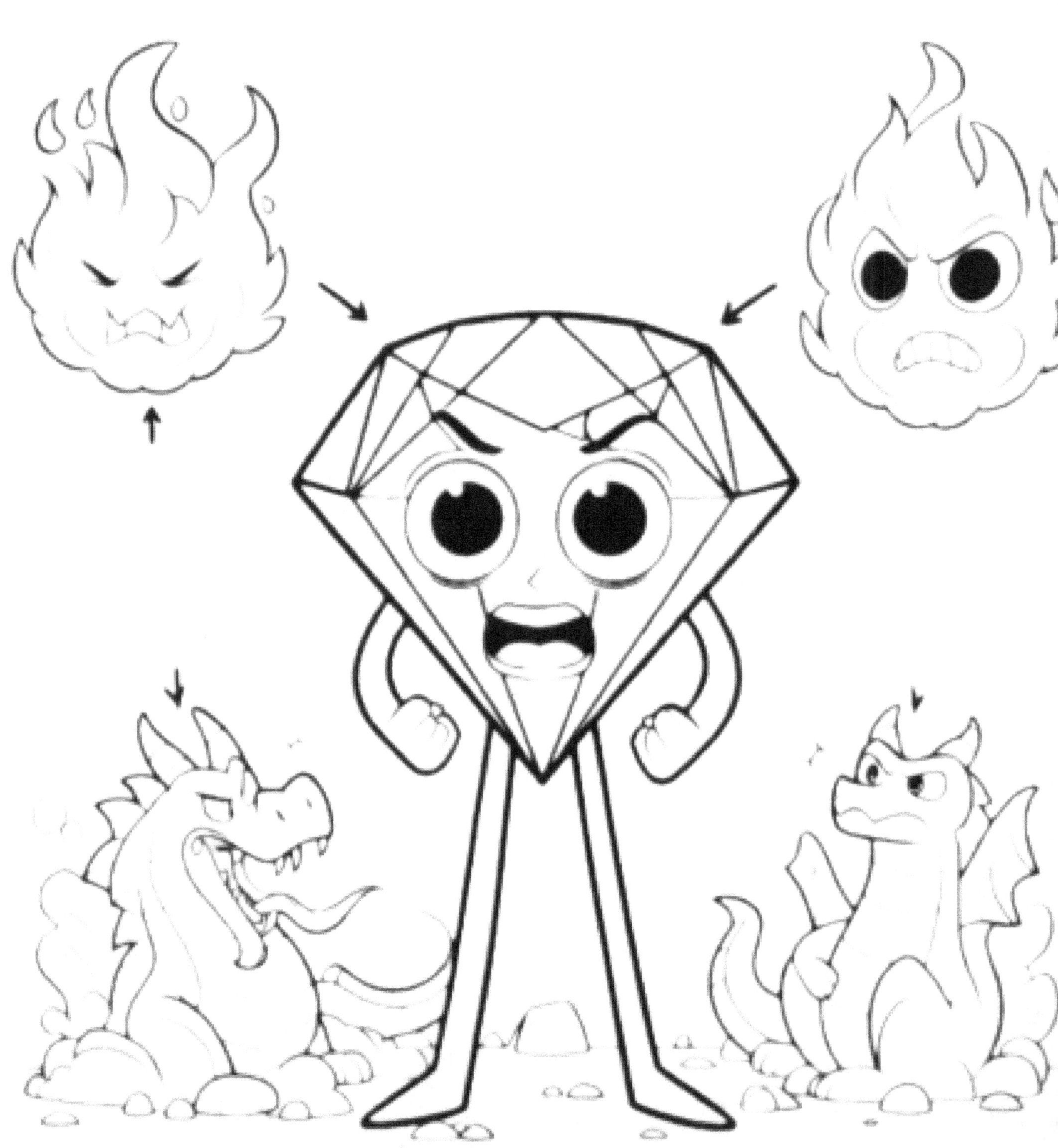

Yay, Brilhante managed to understand, The emotion of anger. He is now happy, Thank you, little friend, for helping him!

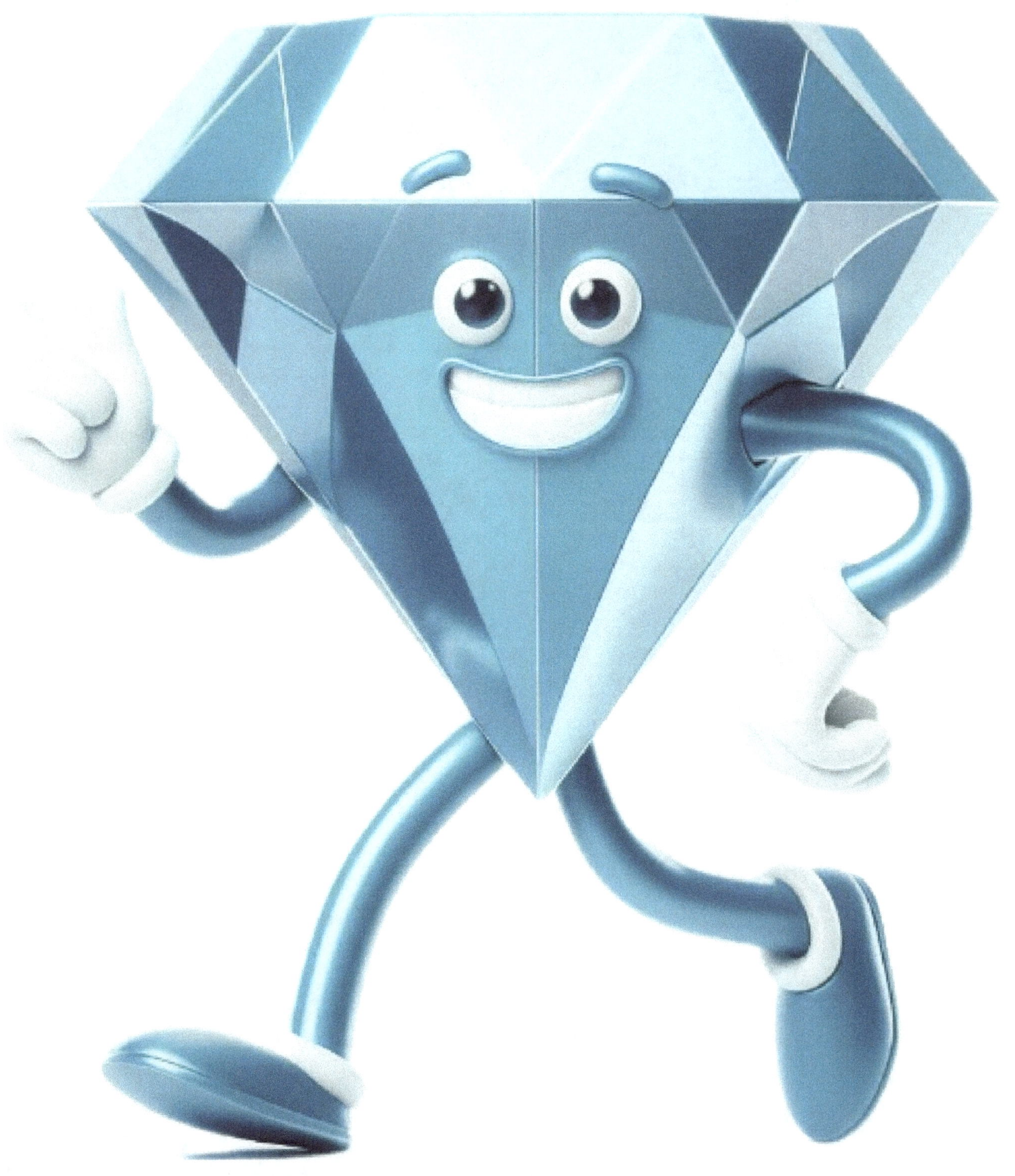

Now it's your turn! Make a drawing to represent Sometimes you felt angry.

Continuing his journey, Brilhante encountered a goblin called Disgust, which introduced him to disgust and repugnance. These emotions were strange to Bright, but he understood that they served to protect and preserve its integrity

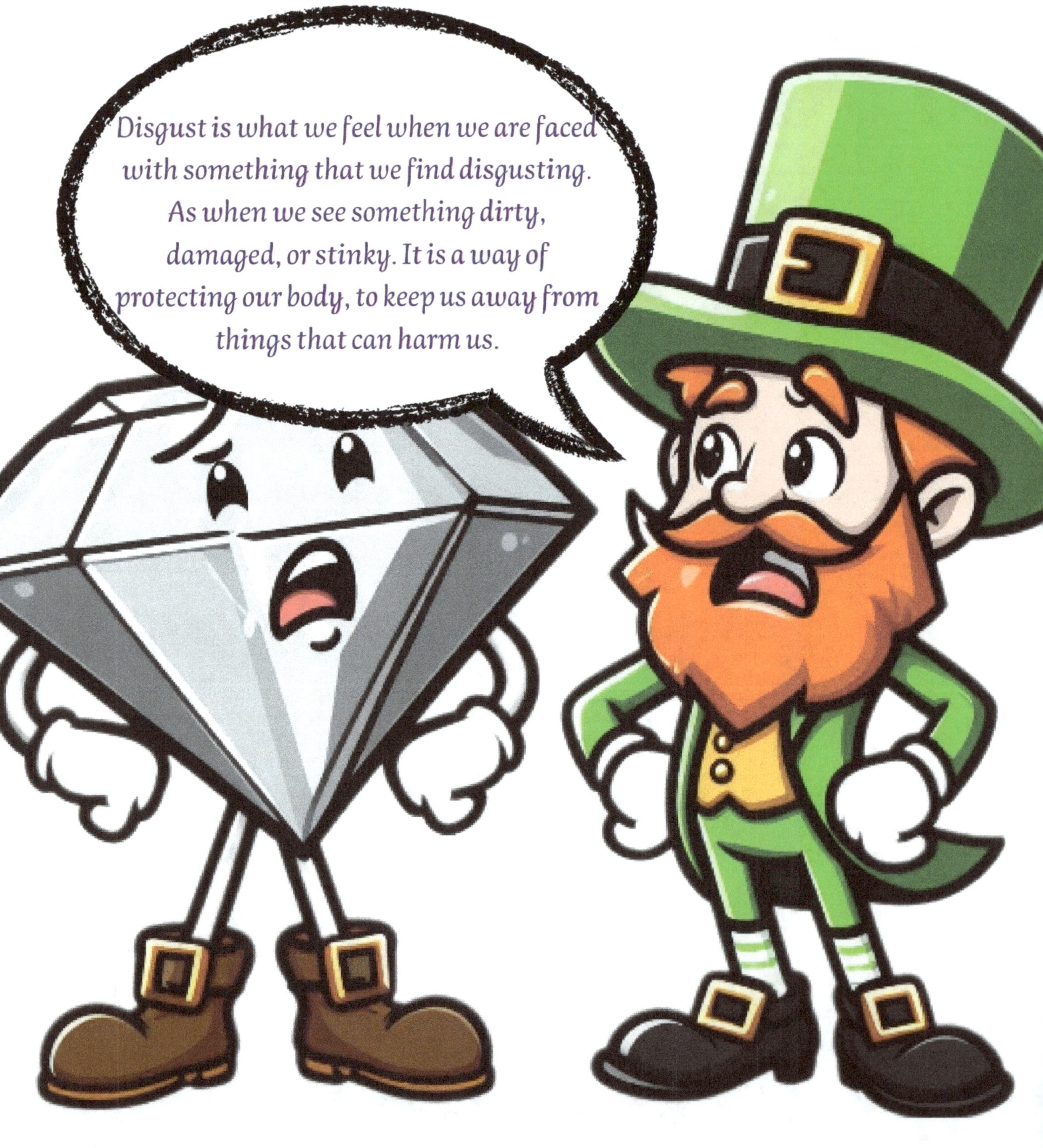

Now Brilliant is understanding Emotion "Disgust" Let's color!

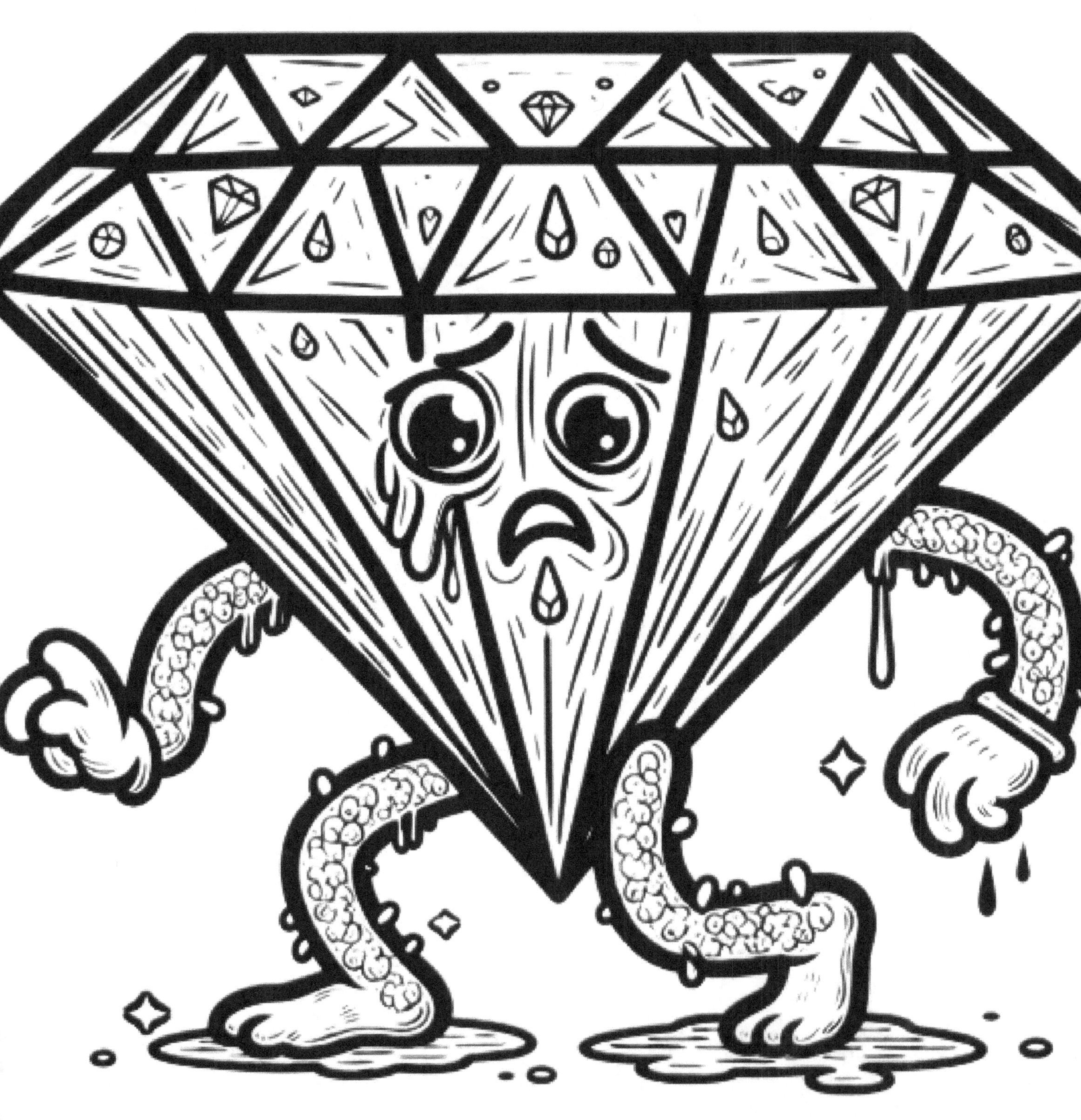

Now Brilliant is understanding Emotion "Disgust" Let's color!

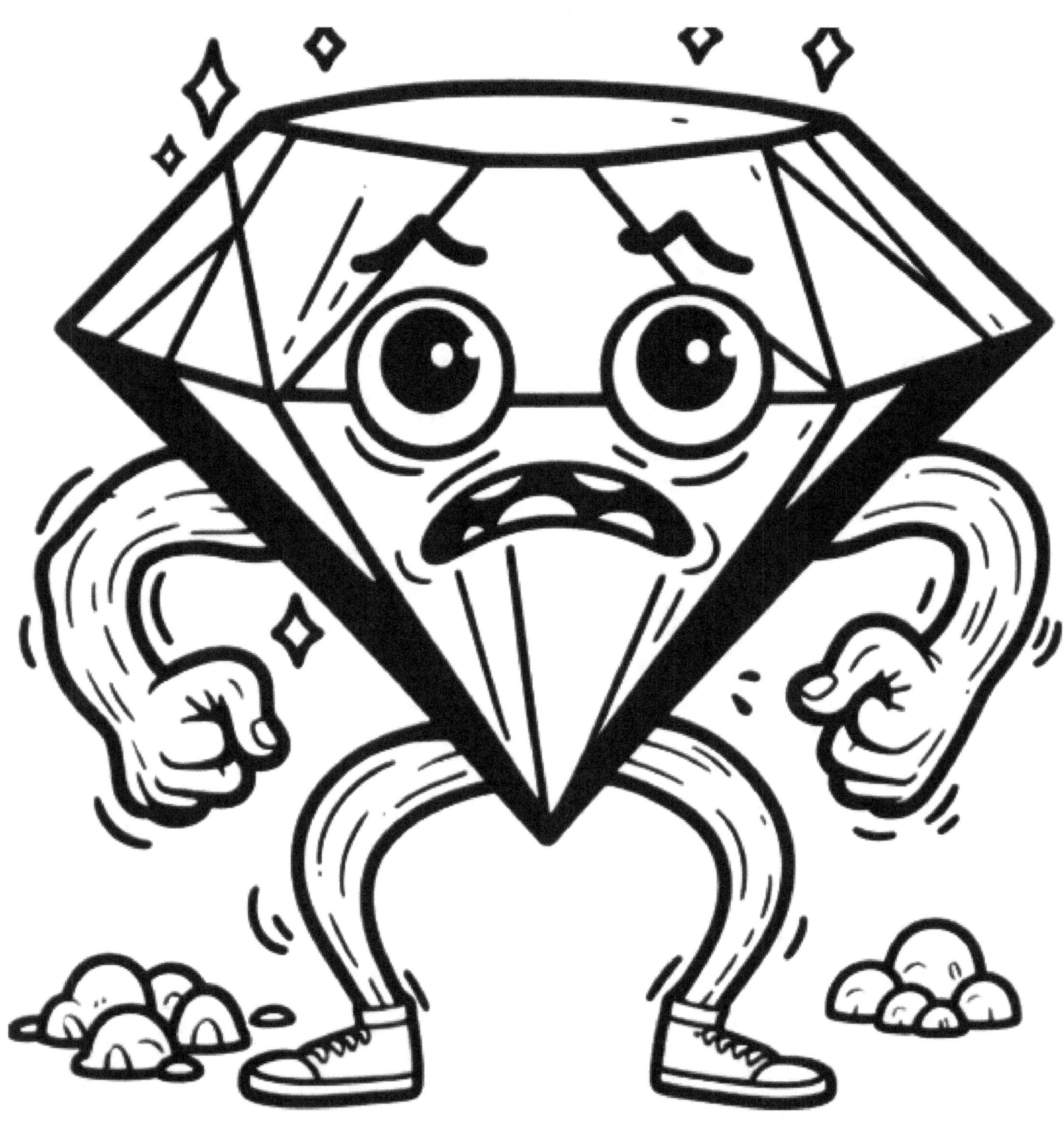

Now Brilliant is understanding Emotion "Disgust" Let's color!

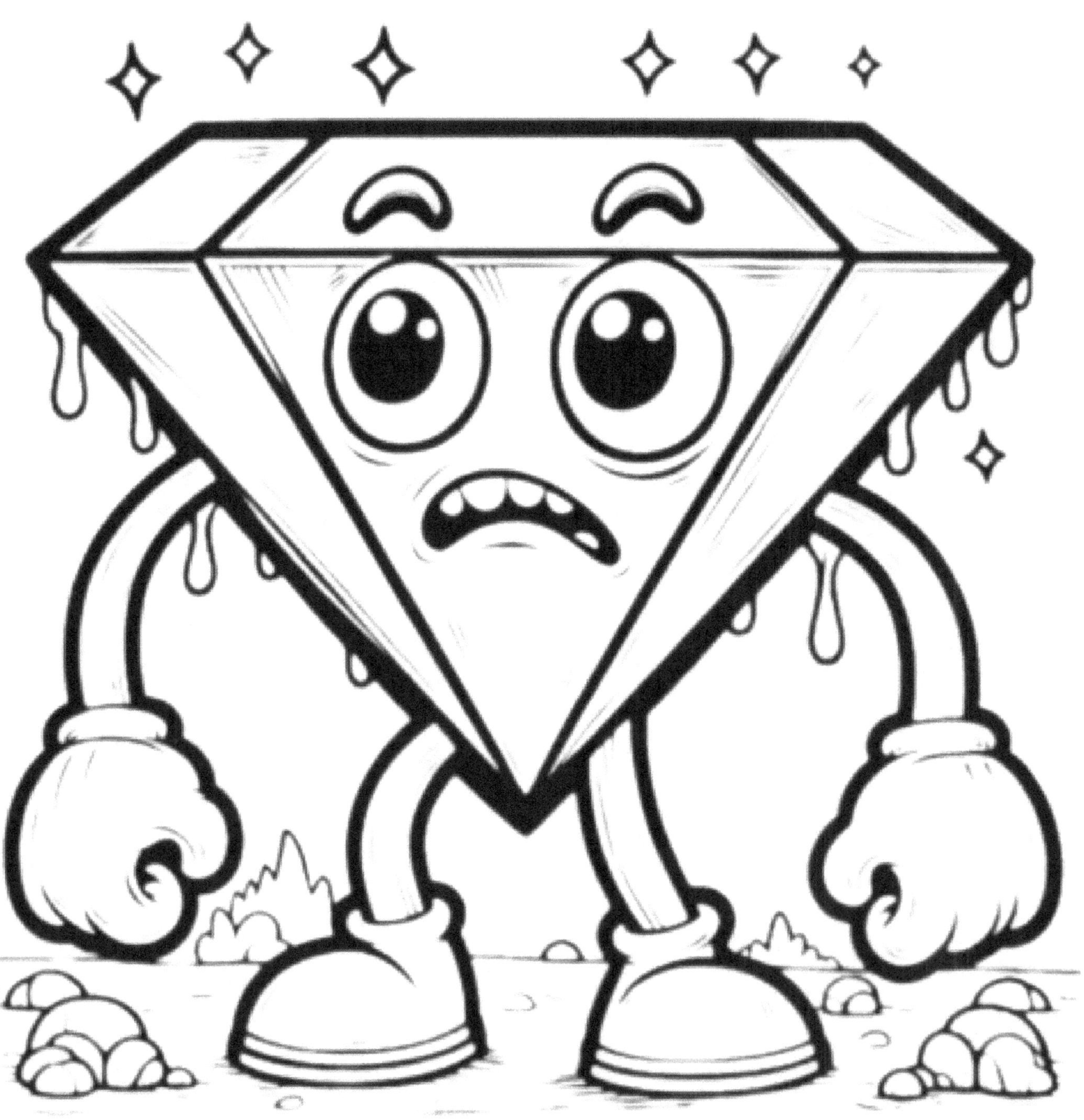

Now Brilliant is understanding Emotion "Disgust" Let's color!

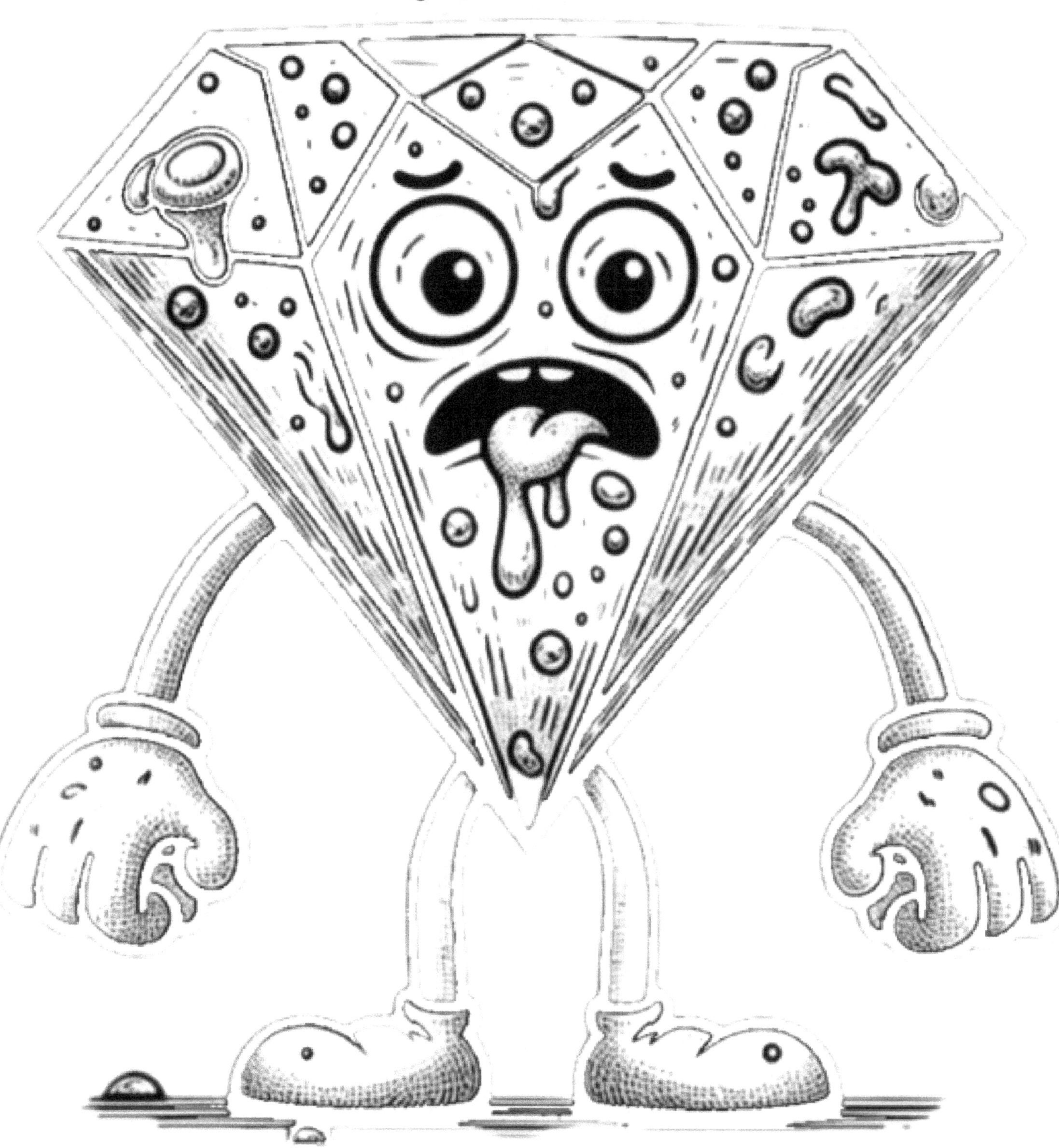

Now Brilliant is understanding Emotion "Disgust" Let's color!

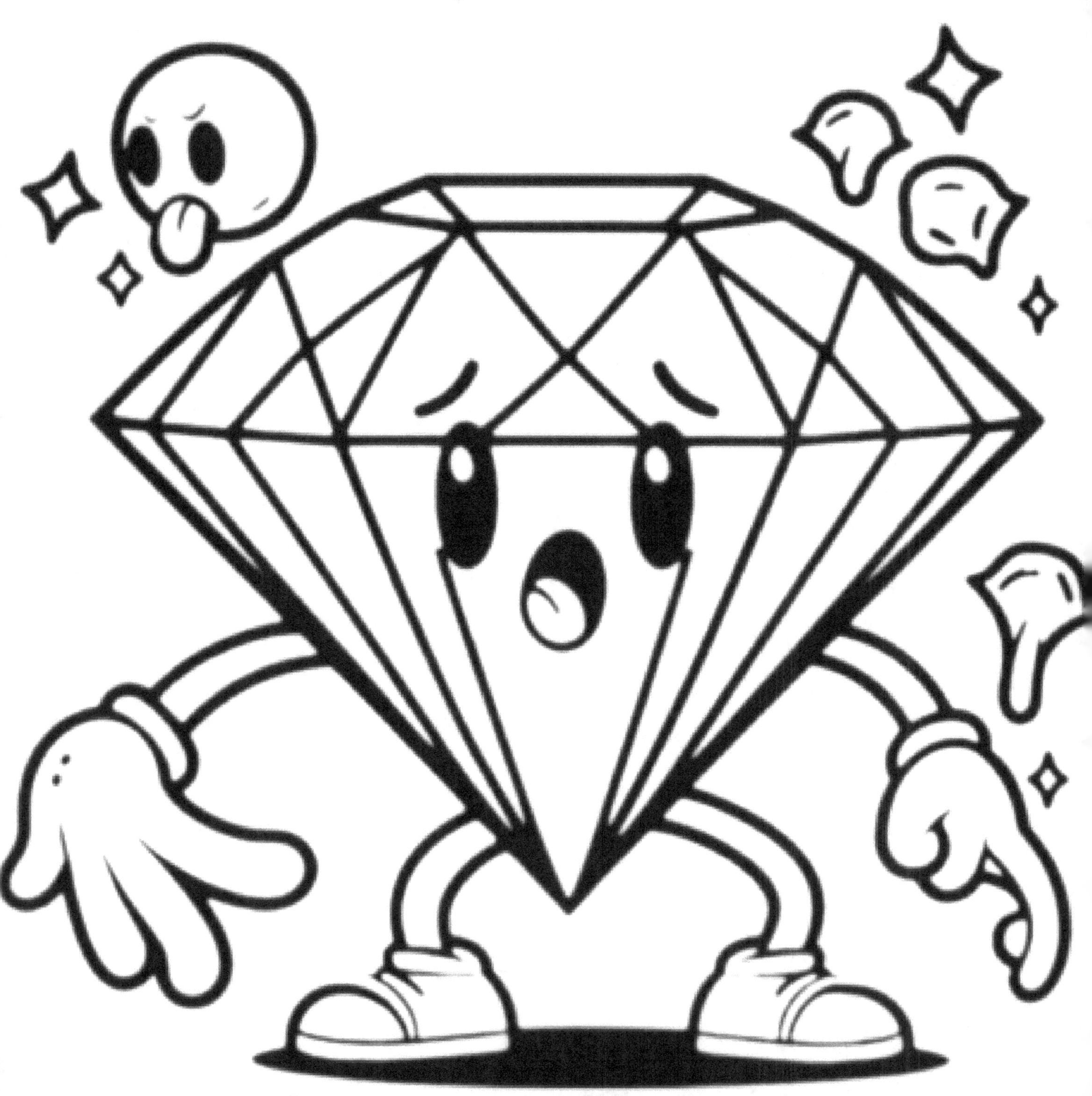

Now Brilliant is understanding Emotion "Disgust" Let's color!

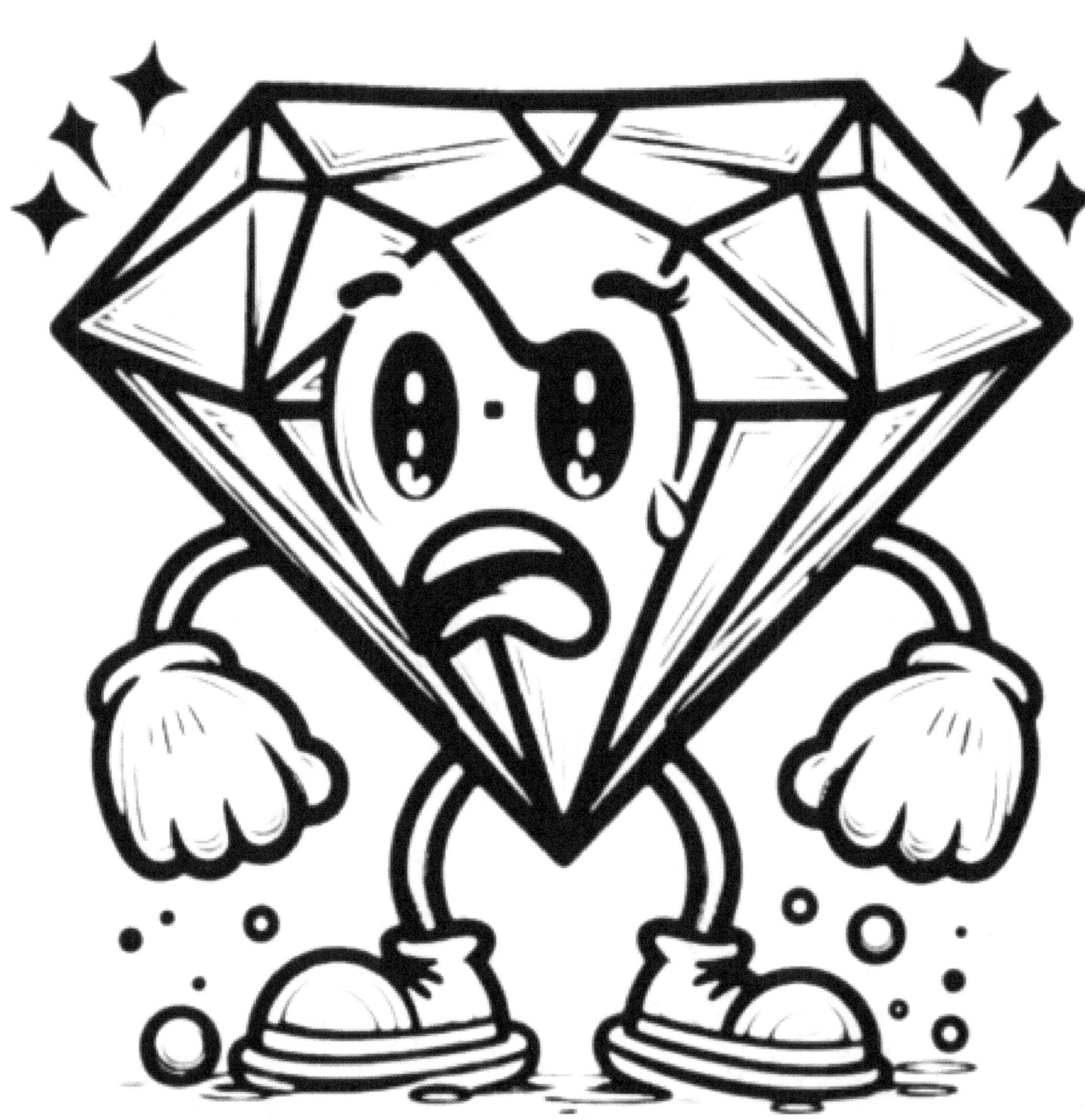

How incredible, Brilliant managed to understand, The emotion of disgust, he is now happy. Thank you, little friend, for helping him!

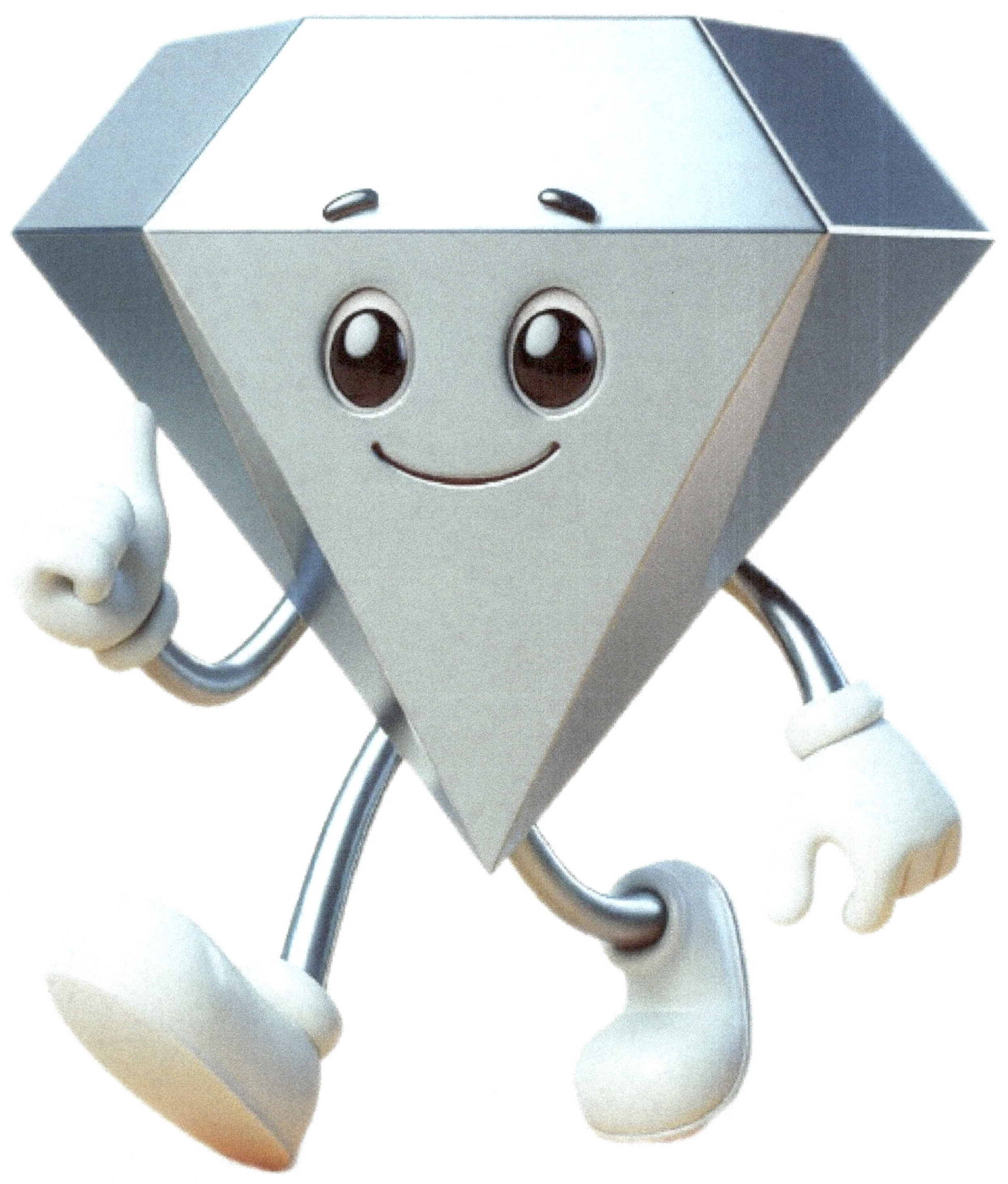

Drawing time! Draw a drawing to describe a situation in which you felt disgusted.

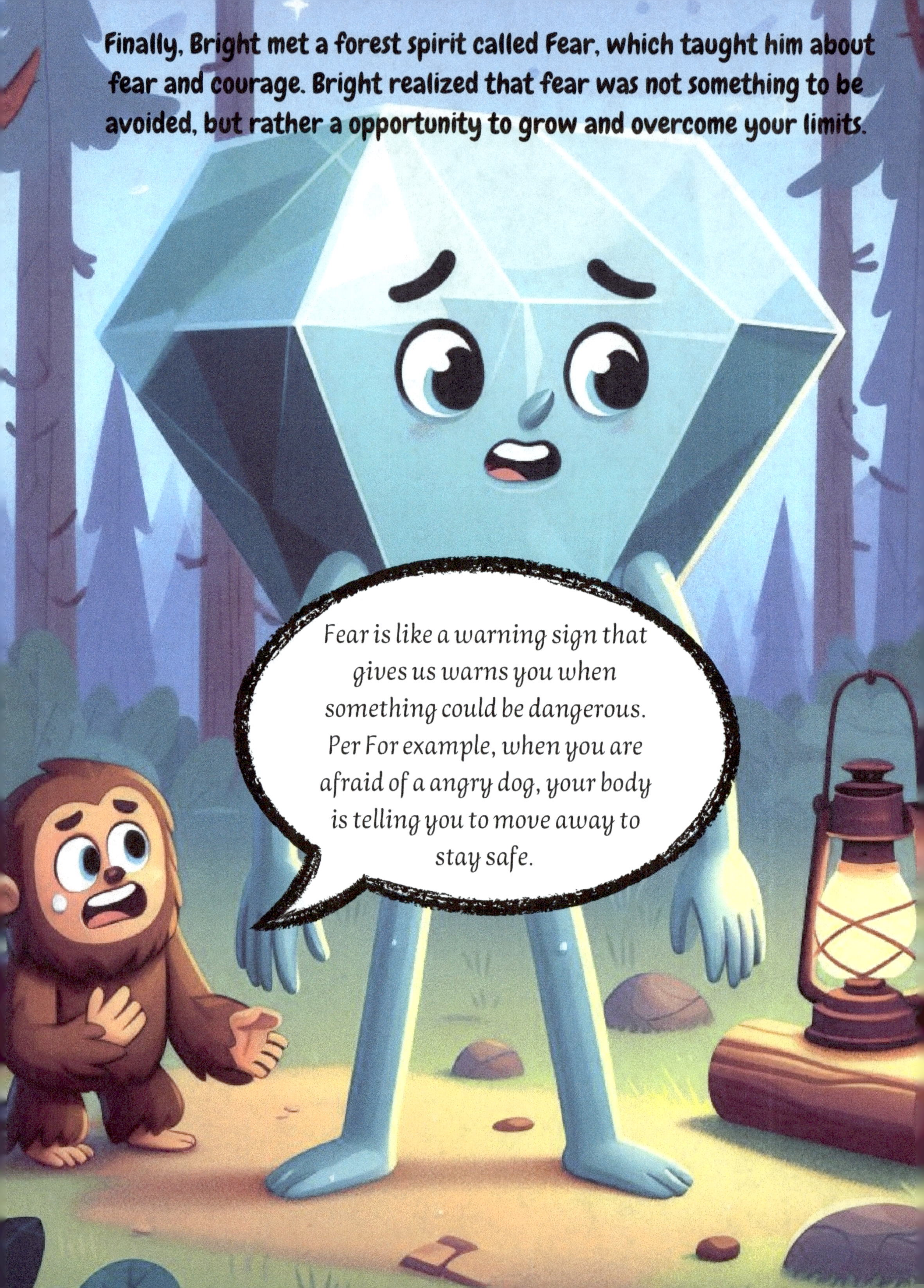

Finally, Bright met a forest spirit called Fear, which taught him about fear and courage. Bright realized that fear was not something to be avoided, but rather a opportunity to grow and overcome your limits.
Fear is like a warning sign that gives us warns you when something could be dangerous. Per For example, when you are afraid of a angry dog, your body is telling you to move away to stay safe.

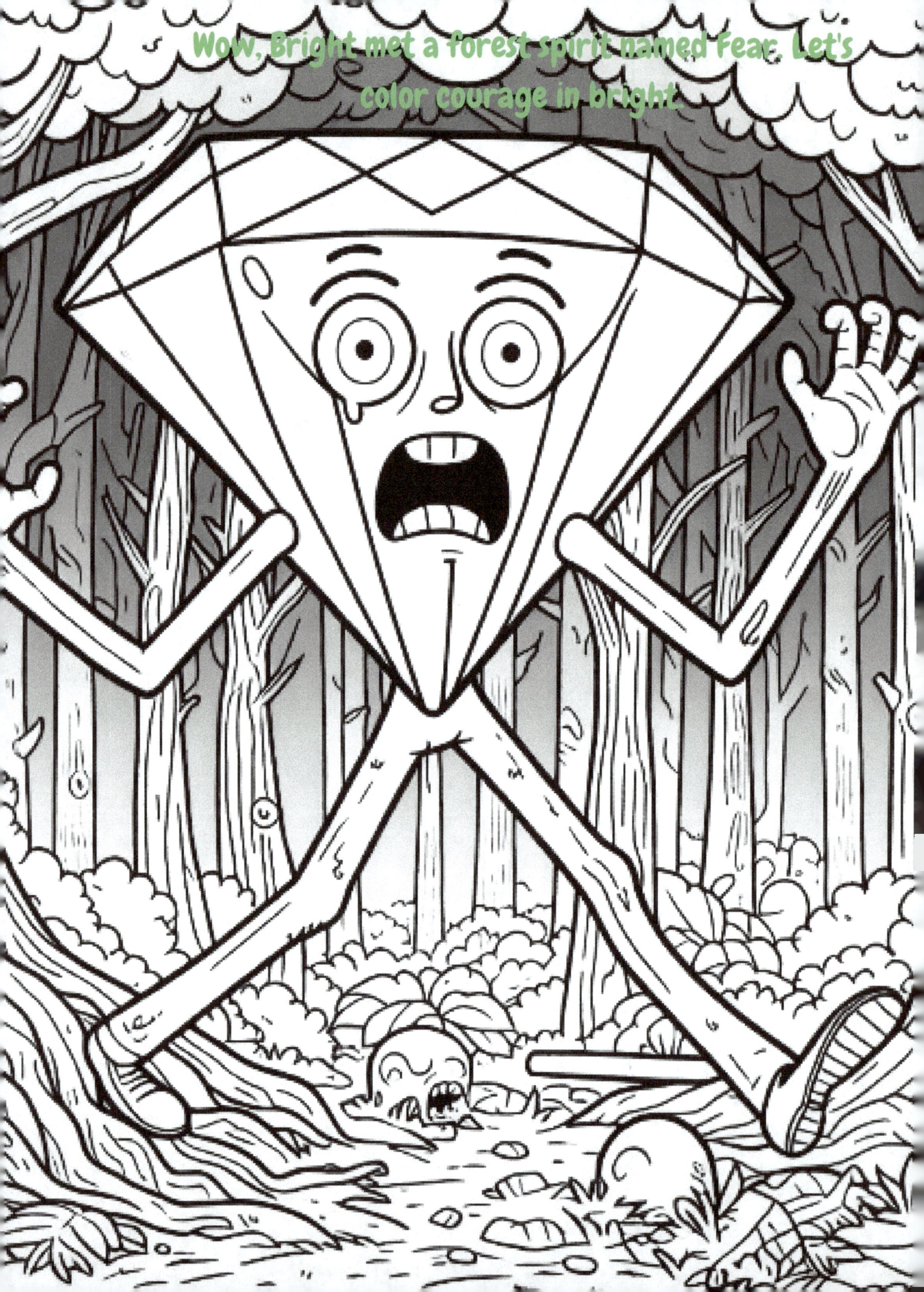
Wow, Bright met a forest spirit named Fear. Let's color courage in bright

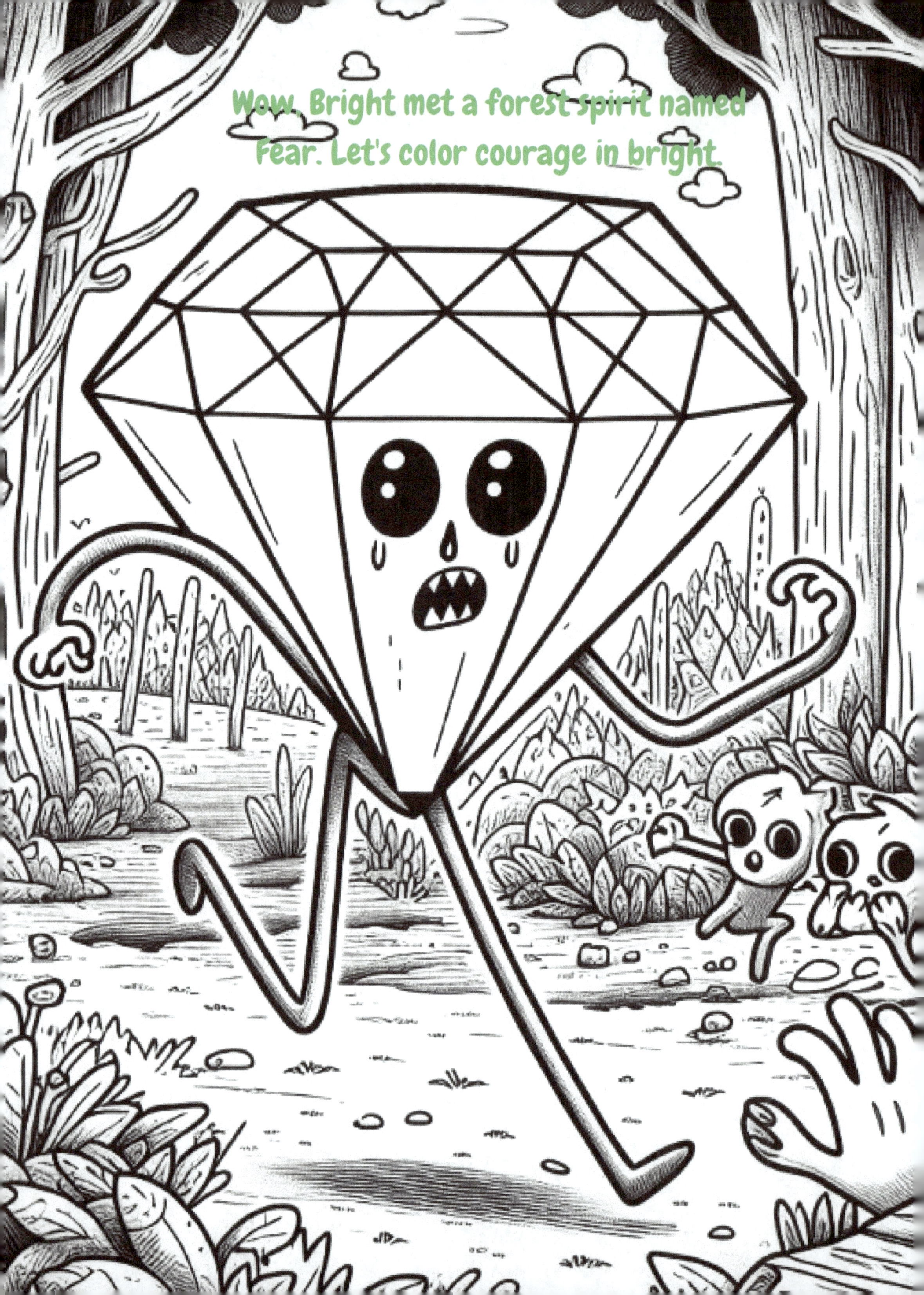
Wow, Bright met a forest spirit named Fear. Let's color courage in bright.

Wow, Bright met a forest spirit named Fear.
Let's color courage in bright.

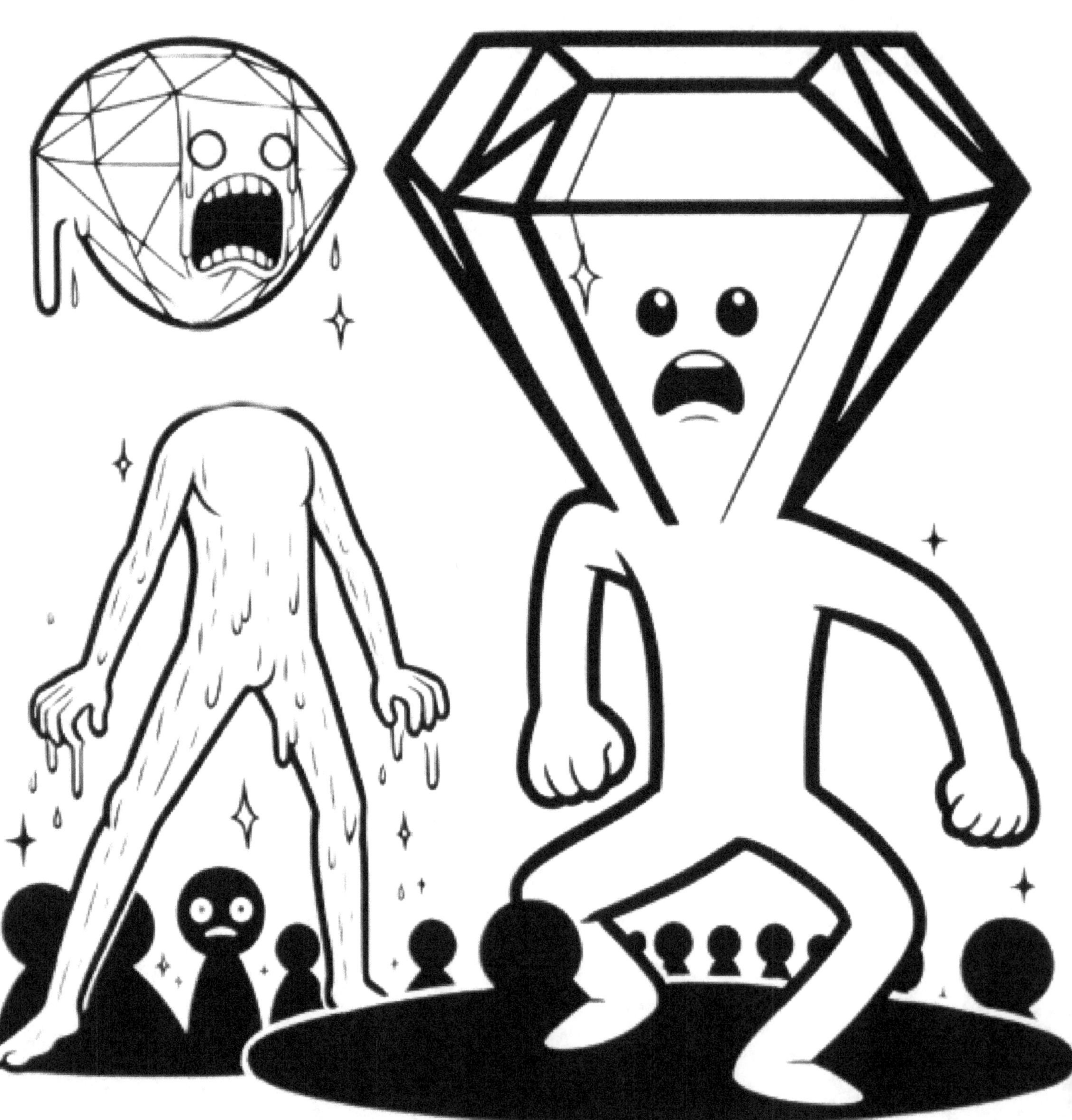

Wow, Bright met a forest spirit named Fear.
Let's color courage in bright.

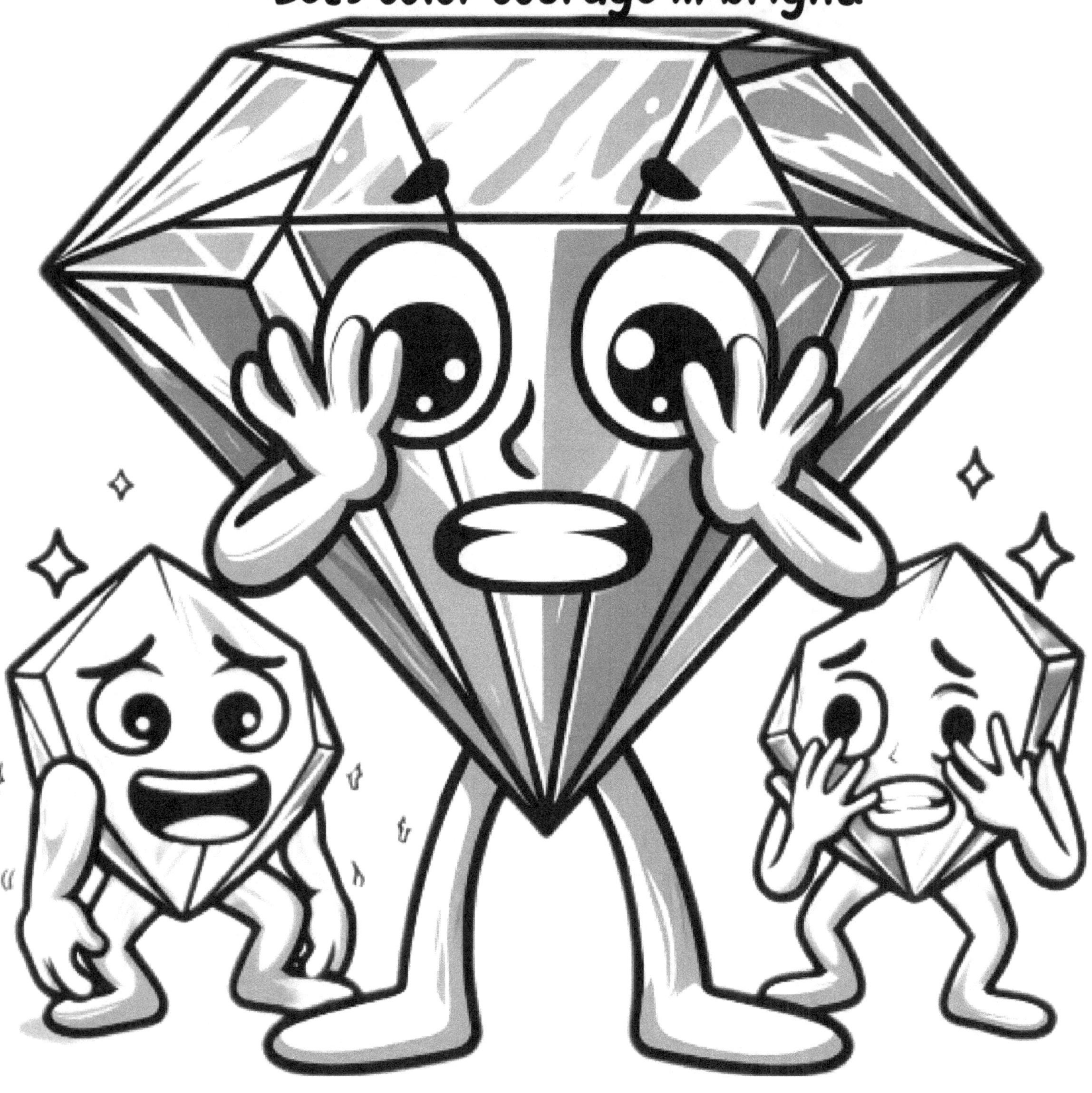

Wow, Bright met a forest spirit named Fear.
Let's color courage in bright.

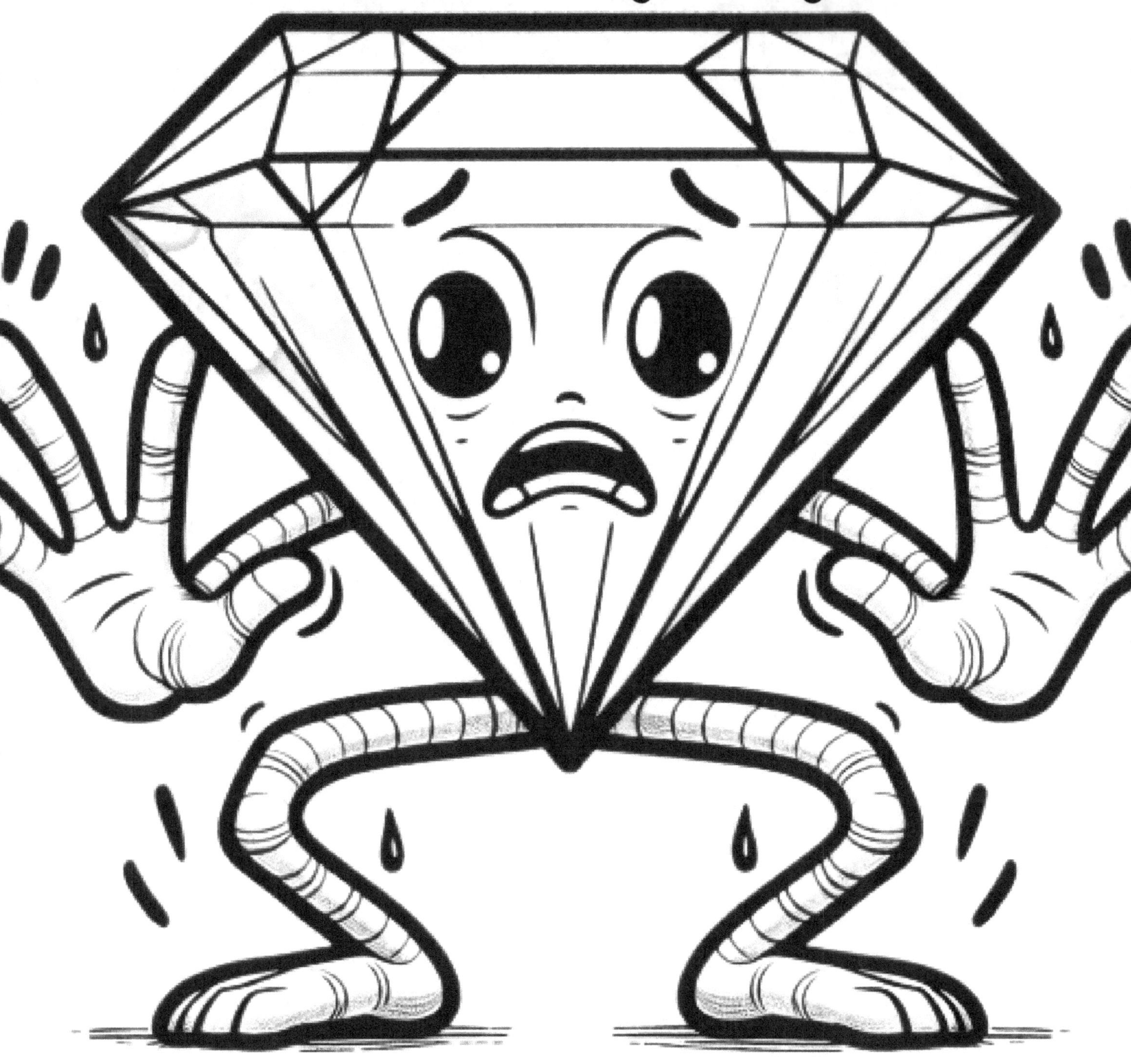

Wow, Bright met a forest spirit named Fear.
Let's color courage in bright.

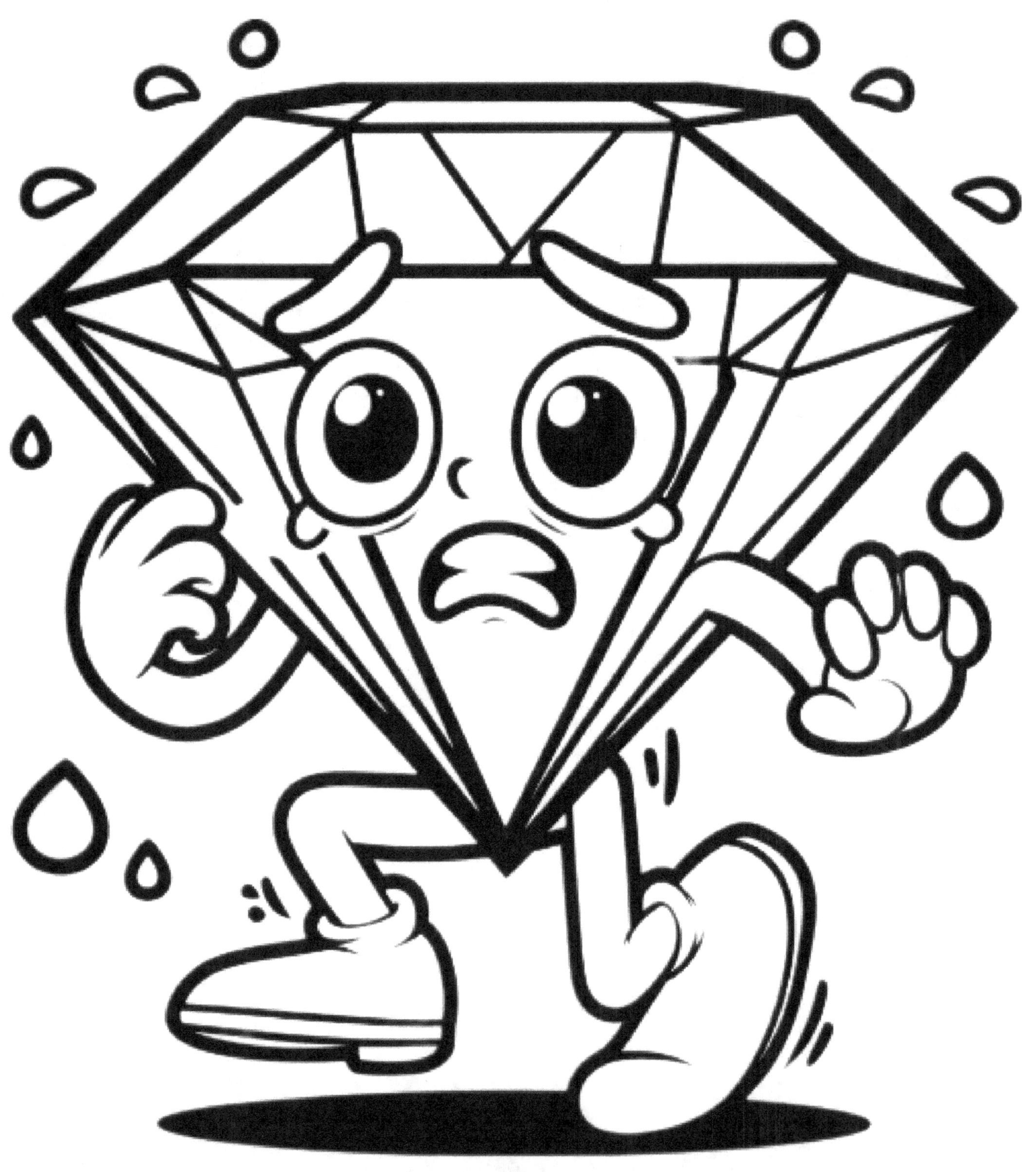

Magnificent, Brilliant managed to understand, The emotion of fear. He is now full of courage. Thank you, little friend, for helping him!

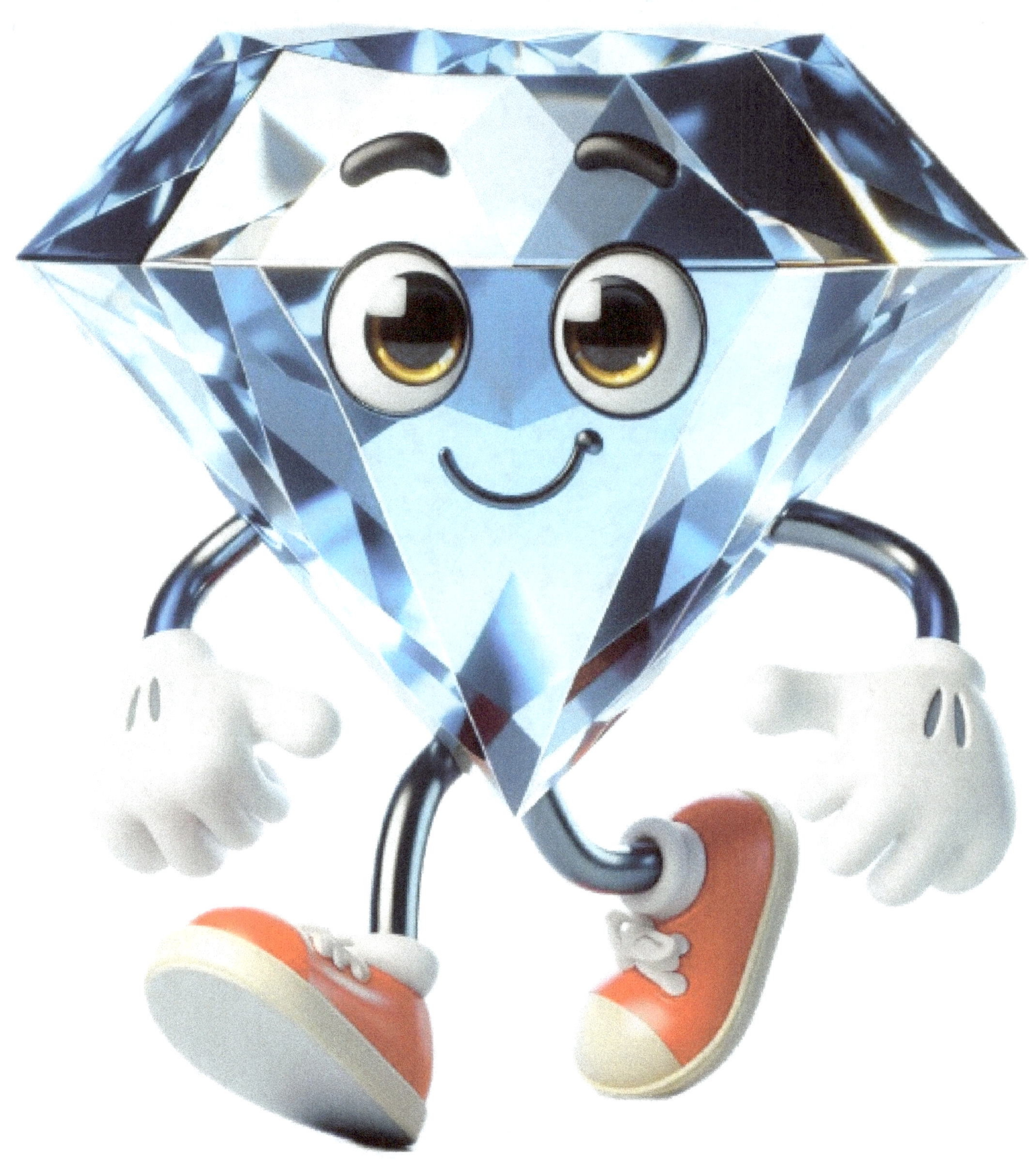

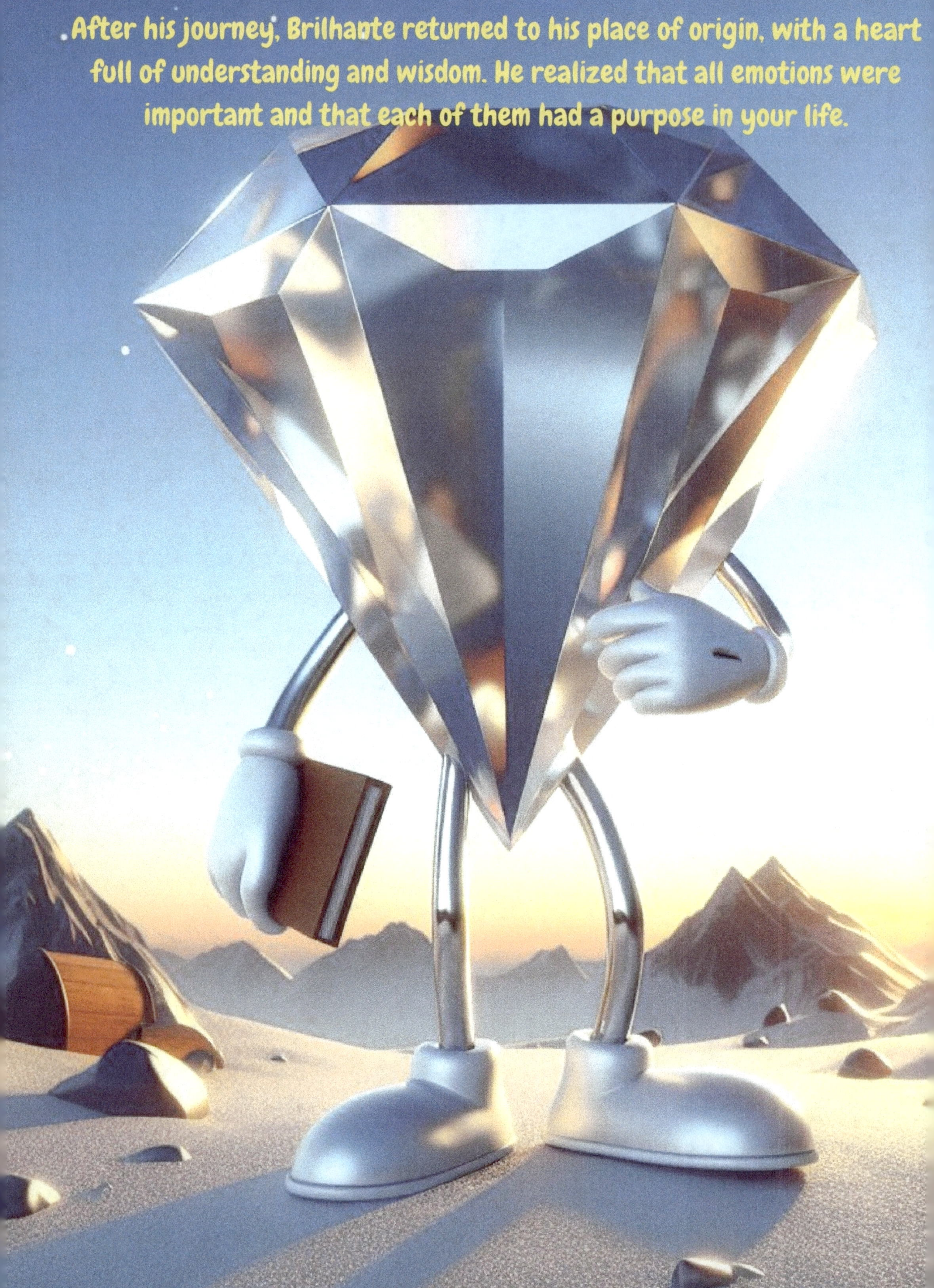
After his journey, Brilhante returned to his place of origin, with a heart full of understanding and wisdom. He realized that all emotions were important and that each of them had a purpose in your life.

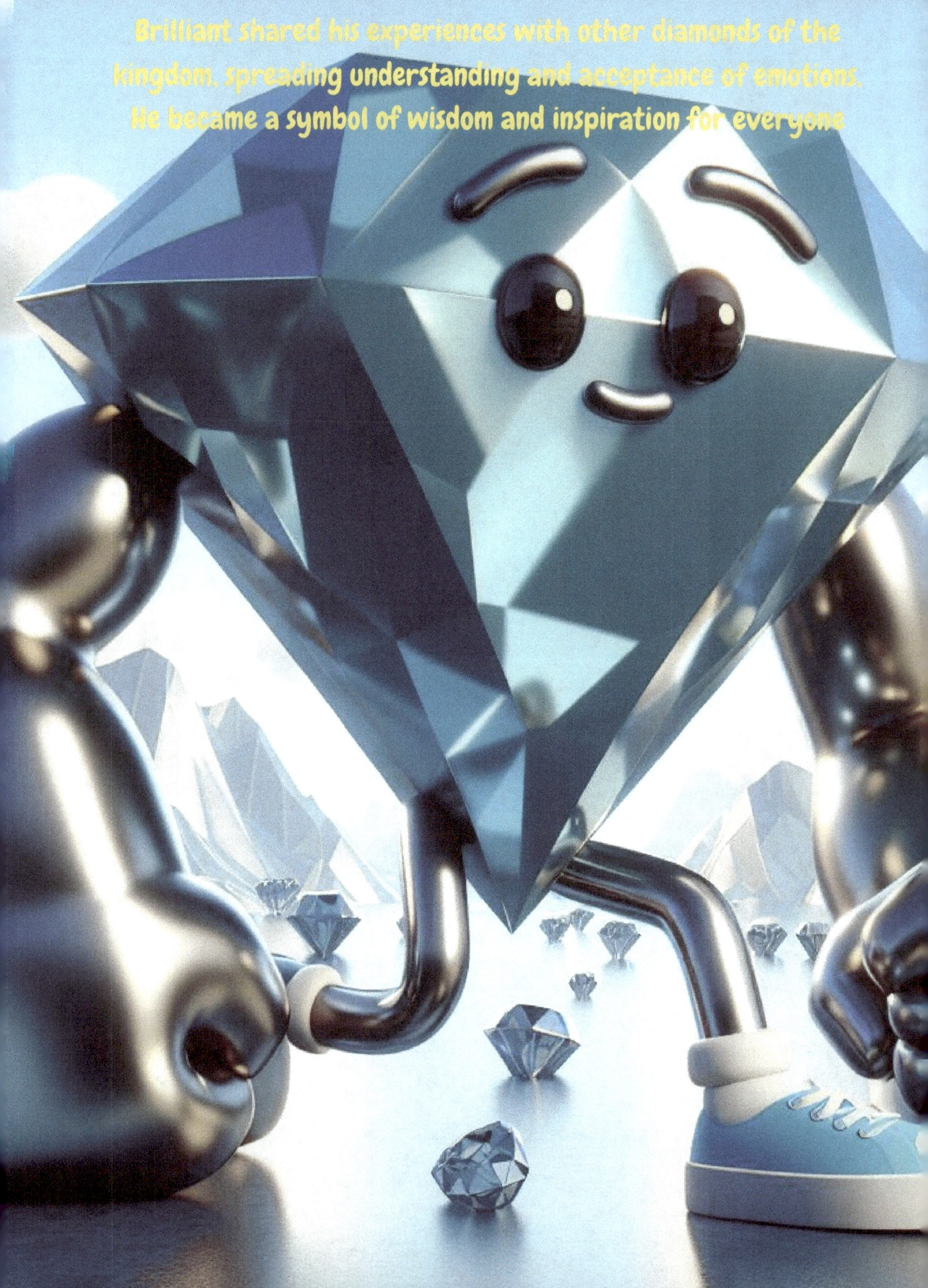
Brilliant shared his experiences with other diamonds of the kingdom, spreading understanding and acceptance of emotions. He became a symbol of wisdom and inspiration for everyone

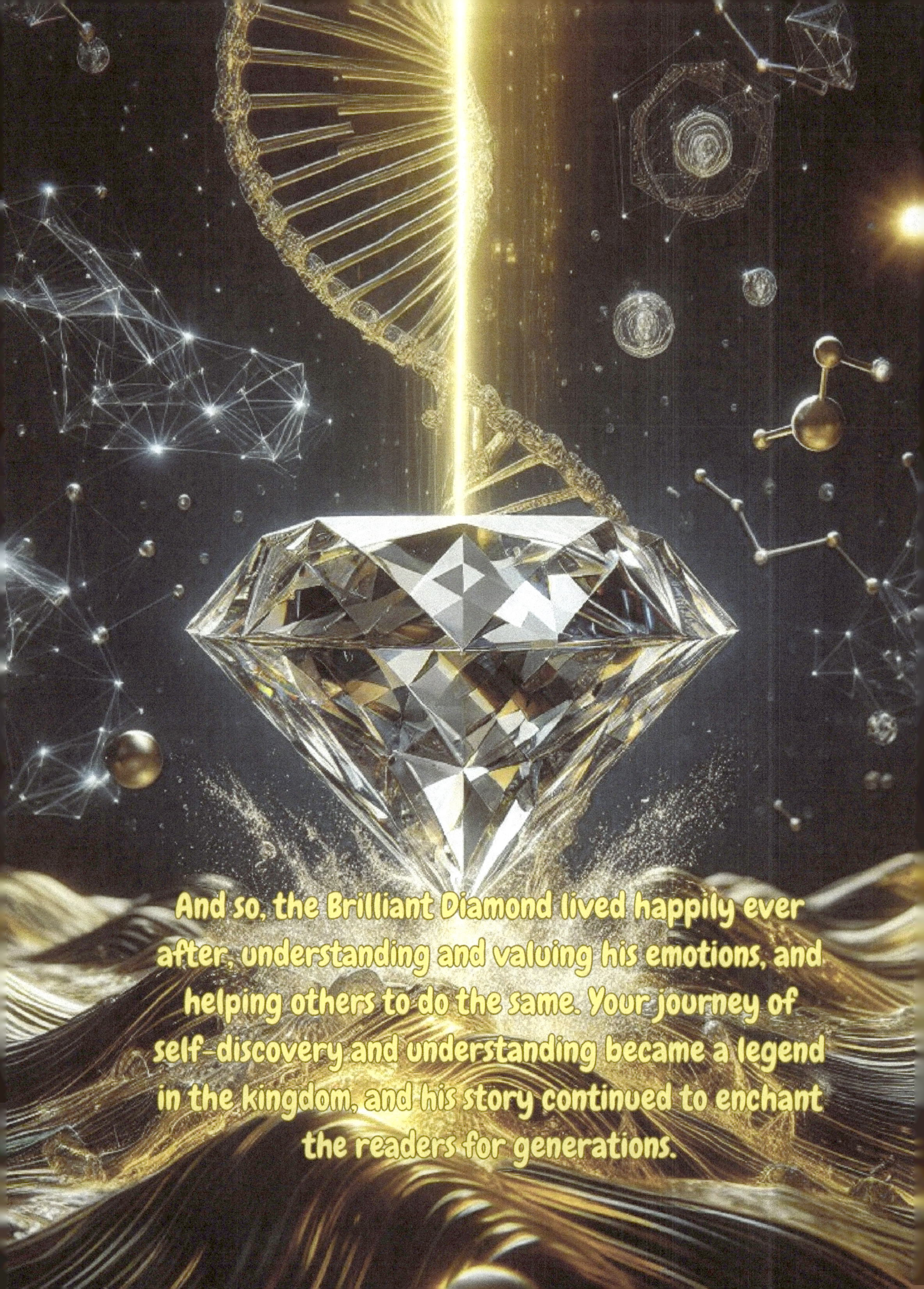

And so, the Brilliant Diamond lived happily ever after, understanding and valuing his emotions, and helping others to do the same. Your journey of self-discovery and understanding became a legend in the kingdom, and his story continued to enchant the readers for generations.

Tell me: What emotion did you enjoy coloring and Which one did you like drawing the most?

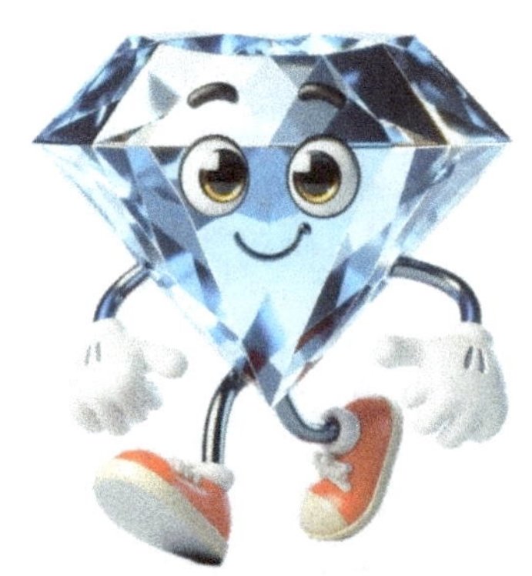

With the book The Art of Coloring Emotions, you helped Brilliant understand that he could express his emotions in creative ways and that in doing so, he became even brighter and more radiant. And so, Brilliant realizes that the true value of a diamond lies not just in its appearance, but in its ability to feel, express and embrace all of its emotions. May this story inspire you, dear reader, to explore your own emotions and consider the value each of them brings to your life. Remember that you are like a precious diamond, full of unique colors and emotions, ready to be expressed and shared with the world. May your journey be full of brightness, comfort and love. And may you always remember the priceless value that resides within you.

Big hug,
Eliana Lima
Diamond Trainer